Online
Lifeline

INTERNET SAFETY FOR KIDS...
AND THEIR PARENTS

LAWRENCE FINE

ISBN 10: 1-933817-39-9
ISBN 13: 978-1-933817-39-2

Published in the USA by
Profits Publishing of Sarasota, Florida
http://profitspublishing.com

Table of Contents

Part I

Just for Kids

Foreword

WHO SHOULD READ THIS BOOK

There have been several books and articles written on the topic of internet safety. They include resources for parents, teachers, and responsible website owners to help keep young people safe on the internet. But there has never been a book written just for you. There has never been a book teaching young people how to keep themselves safe, resources for them to use.

This book is written with one goal in mind. That is, to keep you safe on the internet; to keep you from becoming the latest "Breaking News" story, or the latest "Amber Alert". Everyone knows about the dangers in general, whether it be identity theft, stalking, or getting lured into a bad situation. But few people really sit down and calculate the risks involved with giving out or using the information on the internet.

How often in your daily life do you really stop before you enter your email address on a website, and think "I wonder where this goes?" How often do you do a background check on people you are chatting with? Most people know all of this information, and yet don't put it into practice on a daily basis. It is like knowing where the bad neighborhoods are, but preferring to risk walking alone at night wherever is most convenient.

That is why this book was written. To protect you, to protect your family, and to protect those you know from the dangers of the World Wide Web. To make you aware of the real risks involved in activities most of us participate in without even thinking. To save you from learning the dangers first hand. Once reading this book, you should know what to avoid and how to avoid it. Most importantly, you should know what to do if you or a friend becomes an internet victim.

There are two primary reasons that you should be reading this book. Your main reason for reading is undoubtedly so that you are aware of the dangers and risks involved with activity on the internet, and how to avoid becoming a victim yourself. But, you should also read this book so that you can spot the danger signs that friends and family may show when participating in these activities.

Throughout this book, along with tips to avoid becoming a victim, the warning signs of a potential victim will be described. If you or someone you know is exhibiting these signs, you need to tell a responsible adult right away. It doesn't have to be a parent, a teacher, or even a counselor. It can even be an older sibling. The most important thing is that the adult you trust can take the action required to protect you. If this book can make just one person aware of these risks, it really can make a difference.

This book contains the term "internet crime" more than once, and there is a very specific reason for this. Most of the dangerous activities warned about in this book are actually illegal to participate in. Those who commit these "internet crimes" can be subject to punishment by law, consisting of fines, a criminal record, house arrest, and even jail time. It is important to remember that victims of internet crimes are just that, victims. Just like the victims of other crimes, they often go unheard. Don't be a statistic. If you or someone you know is a victim of an internet crime, tell someone! Some of us may remember our parents telling us, "It isn't you I don't trust, it's everyone else." And that is especially true of the internet. When you are online, if you become the victim of an internet crime, you are not at fault, and you are not a criminal. You are a victim, and you have rights.

There are a few important resources that must be noted here. If you become the victim of an internet crime, and you don't feel comfortable telling your parents or teachers, there are other people who can help you. Your school counselors may be able to offer some help, and even some counseling. If your school has a Police Liaison Officer, talk with them about internet safety. Some schools even have a student council dedicated to internet safety that you can talk to about your problems. If your school doesn't have one, talk to your principal about starting this group. You could be more helpful than you realize.

Go on reading remembering one thing. Although this book warns of the most common dangers on the internet, it couldn't possibly contain them all. Use your common sense, and don't do anything if it doesn't feel right. You are a member of the most advanced society human-kind has ever created. You have infinite resources available at your disposal. Remember that with great power comes great responsibility, and you have a responsibility to be a law abiding and careful internet user. If you take this responsibility seriously, the internet will be a safer place for everyone.

Happy reading, and stay safe.

The Truth - Fact or Fiction?

The reliability of information on the internet

THE MIS-INFORMATION SUPER HIGHWAY

Who could have imagined five or ten years ago how much the internet would become a part of our daily lives. The encyclopedia is now a website, the card catalog is a search engine, and telephone conversations have all but been replaced with instant messengers. The library, while still a good source for information, is no longer the first resource of choice for many of us. With the vast array of information available at our fingertips, 24 hours a day 7 days a week, you have the incredible power to find out in seconds what would have taken hours of research before. However, with this great power comes a great responsibility.

With this fountain of information available to us, it has become our responsibility to distinguish the truth from fiction. The internet is full of information, and not all of it is as reliable as some would have you believe. You don't have to look very far to find fiction masquerading as fact, or vice versa. In fact, look no farther than your favorite search engine. But it can be very difficult to tell fact and fiction apart in some cases. This first chapter is all about the answers to, and the risks of, this significant problem.

Once upon a time, when our parents were writing papers for science class or social studies, they had printed resources. One of the benefits of these resources is that they were screened. People hand-picked these resources, verified their reliability, and put their stamp of approval on them. The library essentially had two sections; One fact, the other fiction. They were very distinguishable, and very easy to tell apart.

Now, the lines between fact and fiction are not nearly as clear-cut as they were. There is no "fact" section on the internet. No one is there to read every website, and make sure that the content is reliable. Websites aren't "hand-picked" to be allowed on the internet. It is up to us to decide whether what we are reading is the truth.

Misinformation takes many forms. Sometimes it may not seem like fiction. Many websites present their information in an "article" format, similar to that in a newspaper. Sometimes it may appear to be far from the truth, when it is in fact based on sound reasoning and is a verifiable fact. Other times it may appear to be a perfect reference for a homework assignment, when in reality it is a collection of made-up facts.

There are several types of misleading websites on the internet. One example would be the "hate site". For everyone who loves a product, theory, or idea, there is someone opposed to it. These sites are very easy to distinguish, as often you will only see negative content about the subject. There may be the occasional defense, in the case of a public forum, but the majority of the content will reflect negatively on the subject. If everything on the website appears to be negative in nature, and contains mostly general comments, chances are that you are viewing a "hate site".

Just the opposite of "hate sites", "fan sites" are websites that are overly optimistic or positive about the subject. Many celebrity fan sites are personal websites, designed and developed by one individual or group to simply share their praise for a certain celebrity. More often than not, however, fan sites are simply websites designed by businesses to promote their products or services. Just like with hate sites, if everything on the website is overly positive, you are most likely viewing a fan site.

Another example of a misleading website would be a commercial website. Many of these are simply advertisements disguised as valuable content. These sites are actually easier to be fooled by, because some companies spend millions of dollars researching how to make the website work best on consumers like you. These are similar to fan sites, but have some similarities to hate sites as well. Often, with a commercial website, you will see a lot of positive information about the product (either specific, like brand names, or in general, like "candy is good", etc.) followed by a lot of negative information about the alternatives (yet again, either specific of general. i.e. "fruit is bad.")

One type of misleading website has actually been around in some form long before the existence of the internet. There are so many of these websites on the world wide web now that it is getting harder to believe any health information found on the internet. Scammers have a huge advantage now with the internet, in that they have a new and more efficient way of reaching their targets. The main thing to remember about sites like this is that if it sounds too good to be true, then it probably is. Nothing that is worth your time can be sped up with money.

Personal opinions are another common type of misinformation site. After all, the internet is essentially a network of people sharing information. When people share information, it is usually biased in some way towards their own personal opinions. Most personal opinion websites are individuals' personal websites, where they post information that they believe or want others to believe. More recently, the advent of blogs has made it even easier to find personal opinion sites on the internet. Blogging has made it easy for anyone who can send an email to have their voice heard, even if their voice isn't the most reliable source for information.

Parody or spoof sites are another common category of misleading websites. Typically a search for any current events will bring up several spoof or parody websites, mocking either the subject of the current event or the individuals involved. These websites are intentionally misleading, although not intended to be harmful. Usually parody or spoof sites are created either for fun as a joke, or to make a political point about a current event. Occasionally, however, parody or spoof sites are created simply to prove how easy it is to fool someone on the internet.

The final category of misleading information is the email hoax. Every one of us has received an email hoax, except maybe for those of us living under a rock. These are often chain letters, forwarded from one friend to another. They often consist of urban legends, false virus or health warnings, or scams about making easy money. These are particularly easy to spot, because they usually have some kind of ridiculous claim attached to them. Once again, if it sounds too good to be true, it probably is.

The risks of using the information from these sites vary in severity, but they all do carry risks. If used for homework, you can fail your assignment or even the whole class. If used to make important decisions, you could make the wrong decision, and anything could happen. It is important to take information you find on the internet in context, and as your mother always said, "consider the source."

There are few warning signs that someone is being led on by misleading information, other than the obvious act of telling you something that you know isn't true. But there are some things to watch out for. For example, if your friend seems uncontrollably excited about something they read on the internet, but are incredibly secretive, they may be the victim of an email hoax. Often after a few days, your friend will no longer be interested in discussing their internet secret. This is a good sign, because it means they have discovered that it was a hoax.

Remember not to be discouraged about information on the internet. There are ways to safeguard against misinformation. First, always double check your sources. Once you find the fact you are looking for, go to your favorite encyclopedia site (such as Wikipedia.com) and double check the information. Check if your source is credible. Do they post contact details online? Do they have a disclaimer on their website about their information? Are you using an online encyclopedia, or someone's personal website? Can you verify the information you've found using the information on other websites? When was this website last updated? Is there a place other than the internet you can use to confirm this information? All of these are important questions to ask when using information found on the internet, as they can save you from tremendous amounts of hassle.

Misinformation on the internet is no joke, it is a real problem. If it isn't recognized early, there can be serious consequences to using the information. Be careful when researching on the internet, and if you get discouraged, remember that there is always the public library. Use your judgment, and always double check your sources elsewhere. You will save yourself a lot of time and headache.

Phish Tales

When good people let bad things happen

PHISHING IS A SERIOUS PROBLEM

Identity theft isn't just an adult problem. Even you can become a victim if you aren't careful. Phishing is when a spammer or other online con-artist pretends that they are your bank, insurance company, or another company with access to your sensitive information. They will often do a very good job of copying graphics, links, and stationary to appear to be "the real thing". The email will then ask you to verify your password, your account number, or some other information that normally the bank would have.

A word of caution; Never, EVER click on the link in that email. If you get an email that you believe may be from your bank or another institution, go directly to their website (the way you normally access it), and report the email. They will usually reply within minutes telling you if the email is a fake or not. Most of the time these emails are false. Remember that your bank or other institution already has this information. They do not need you to confirm it in an email. Also, it may give you tips for protection against these emails right on the website of these companies. Remember that if information is needed from you, your bank or insurance company would never request it through email.

You may be able to tell if you are a target for phishing simply by checking your email. If you start to notice a lot of email from companies you don't deal with, asking to confirm your information, chances are that you are on a mailing list for these scammers. Oftentimes you will even get scam emails from companies that don't exist, such as "Trusted Bank" or "Insurance Inc."

Phishing is a real problem today. Between October 2004 and June 2005, reports of phishing attempts increased more than 100%, from 6957 to 15050. Phishers will often use URLs that look like the appropriate address, but add just enough to redirect you to their phishing site. An example might be www.trustedbank.fake.com. This URL is obviously false, but many phishers will use letters or numbers in place of the word "fake" to look like technical information that you see in many URLs. Some phishers have even gone as far as hacking into legitimate websites and stealing your information if you visit while they have access.

Phishing isn't just limited to email, either. Phishing attacks on users of social networking sites go back to the very early days of the crime, when scammers would attempt to steal AOL passwords using chat rooms and instant messengers. Some experiments have shown a success rate of over 70% for phishing attacks on social networking sites like MySpace; a whopping seven out of ten users who are presented with a phishing scam will enter their information.

The damage caused by phishing is far reaching, and can destroy lives. It can ruin credit, destroy social relationships and leave individuals with trust issues. But there are ways that you can fight back against phishing scams. The easiest way involves simply continuing what you are doing right now, and educating yourself on the signs of phishing scams and the risks involved. You can also watch for signs in your email that what you are viewing may be a phishing scam. Often, email from legitimate companies will contain some kind of personalization; Whether it be your real name, your username, or even a partial account number. Emails with greetings such as "Dear _____ Customer" or "Valued Customers" should be viewed as suspicious. Make sure you have the latest technology installed on your computer to help protect you from phishing. Some newer versions of web browsers actually include a warning that tells you when you visit a potential phishing site. Other new email programs include a warning when you are viewing an email that may be a phishing scam. Don't rely only on these measures, however. A software program is no replacement for common sense.

Hey, I know you!

Your identity and the internet

You're More Popular Than You Think

Identity theft isn't just an adult problem. Even you can become a victim if you aren't careful.

Your identity, especially today, is a valuable item. It is something that no one else has, and that those with ill intentions desire. Treat your identity like a valuable gem. Never show it to anyone, never tell anyone about it, and keep it under lock and key. The more you boast about your identity, the more thieves will want it. You wouldn't go around the internet posting pictures and locations of a precious diamond, don't do it with your identity.

There are a lot more people out there than you think who want your information. Everyone has heard about the problems with identity theft. There are credit cards being forged, bank accounts being hijacked, and peoples' lives being destroyed. But your identity isn't just about your sensitive financial information. Even the youngest internet surfers can be victims of privacy invasions.

There are many ways to get your information using the internet. It only takes one form, one email, one chat room message for your identity to become a fraudster's playground. Things to beware of include filling out surveys & contest entry forms, registering for internet services like email, instant messengers and file-sharing programs, completing a personal profile for your email or instant messenger account, creating a profile on a social networking site like MySpace or Nexopia, or giving information, even just your name or phone number, to people in chat rooms and over instant messenger.

If you do any of these things, chances are that your information is scattered all over the World Wide Web for everyone to see. A recent example is a list of MySpace usernames and passwords that was circulating on the internet. The hackers simply found users on MySpace, got to know them, and asked them an innocent enough question. The question was usually along the lines of "What is your dog's name?" or "What school do you go to?" Unfortunately, the answers to these questions were also the answers to the users' "secret questions", allowing hackers to change the users' passwords and gain full access to their account.

The information you enter in forms online can also be used against you in legal ways. Companies will often purchase the information in bulk, with the intentions of using the information for marketing purposes. In marketing circles, this is known as "co-registration". Essentially, this means that when you sign up to one website, you are signing up to the other website as well, giving the marketer full access to the information in the forms. This information can be used against you, like when a company wants to market their new product to you. They know exactly what you like, where you live, and who you hang out with. This makes it very easy for them to influence you into purchasing without you even knowing it.

There are a lot more risks than marketing messages when

you give your information out over the internet. Cyber-stalking, online bullying and even identity theft can happen. Remember, just because you aren't an adult now doesn't mean you never will be. Someone could use your information and pretend to be you. If they know your age and your birthday, it will be easy for them to know when they can really do damage to your life. Young people with criminal records who are looking to cross borders will often seek the identity information of someone of a similar age who is similar in appearance. You make have the exact likeness of a fugitive, and not even know it. The problem appears when they know it. They will use your identity to cross borders, sign documents, and commit crimes. You could end up with a criminal record because of a young identity thief.

One of the most over-looked ways of protecting your information is actually in front of you every day. For every website on which you use any personal information, read their privacy policy. Most are fairly standard issue, but some are not. These privacy policies are legal documents that companies have spent hundreds, or even thousands of dollars to write up to protect them. The problem is that they don't protect you. There have been cases where the company's privacy policy actually said that they would sell your information, use it for market research, and gather information on your surfing habits. That information is on the website for a reason. When you click agree, you are legally saying "okay" to whatever they just wrote. You wouldn't sign a contract for a job or a purchase without reading it, so why agree to a privacy policy without reading it first? Spending an extra five minutes can save you a lifetime of trouble.

Any Information Is Dangerous

It is obvious that personal information includes things such as your Social Security Number, legal name, address and so forth. But how much information really is personal information. Take, for example, your phone number. You have probably given it to more than one online friend. But, using just your phone number, your online friend could easily find out where you live, what your last name is, who your parents are, and even figure out what school you go to. Giving your phone number to the wrong person is very, very dangerous. If an online predator had your phone number, and got all of the information above, they could very easily come to your school, have you called to the office, and kidnap you right there. Any information is dangerous in the hands of the wrong people.

There are many ways to avoid becoming a victim of identity theft. The most important thing is to always know who you are giving your important information to. Even when you know who is on the receiving end of your information, you should always be sure that you are sending the information over a secure connection. Instant messengers and private messages in chat rooms are not secure. Just because it appears that no one else is watching doesn't make that true. You could have key-logging software installed on your computer and not even know it. You type in something that looks like a credit card number, the key-logger records it, and sends it to an online scam artist. Presto, you are a victim of identity theft.

With all the ways to avoid identity security issues, identity theft can still happen. It is important to recognize the warning signs in your friends and family so that you can help them if they ever become a victim of identity crimes.

Warning signs of identity theft include receiving bills for accounts you didn't open, seeing unauthorized charges on your cell phone bill, bank account or credit card, being contacted by a collection agency for a debt you didn't incur, your bills arriving late suddenly when they have always been on time, or mail disappearing all together.

You should also watch for signs that could indicate one of your friends is participating in identity crimes. Addicts, whether they are drug abusers, alcoholics or gamblers, all have a need for cash and a taste of crime. Watch out for friends living well beyond their means. If your friend works at a fast food restaurant and filed for bankruptcy six months ago suddenly drives up in a luxury SUV, be suspicious. Make sure to change passwords and security information after break-ups or bad fights with friends or boyfriends/girlfriends. Often they have both the means and the motive to wreak havoc on your identity.

The Internet Persona

The new identity crisis

SO-CALLED FREEDOM

The internet isn't like your parents' house or your school's lunch room. There aren't people watching out for you every moment of the day. You don't spend every waking minute with people who know you in and out. It is very easy to say and do whatever you want, or even be whomever you want, when you are on the world wide web.

Many young adults like you think that it is easier to get away with things on the internet. No one can track them down, they are online. Hurting other people on the internet is easy, because you can just hide behind your email address, right? Wrong. An email address, while a marvel of technology, can't simply "hide you" and where you are located. Take a look at the headers in an email, and you will see. They will often include what is called an IP address (IP stands for Internet Protocol). This address can uniquely identify who your internet service provider is, and in turn identify who you are, all with this unique little number.

You cannot hide behind the internet and use it for ill purposes. Many court cases in the United States and around the world have been won because the person who committed a crime used the internet, and therefore their IP address was logged and tracked down. Enforcement agencies such as the FBI, CIA and even local and regional police services have the capability to track down individuals based solely on their IP address. And if, hypothetically speaking, a certain police or enforcement organization were to find themselves unable to track down an individual, they could simply contact the suspected Internet Service Provider (or ISP) and have them tracked down that way.

You shouldn't fear this technology, but rather be glad it exists. It is because of IP tracking technology that you can feel a little bit safer on the internet. If an individual commits a crime on the internet, they can and will be caught, most likely because of IP tracking technology.

Some individuals feel that they are invincible on the internet, because of the anonymity. As you can see from the information above, this is just not true. There is no anonymity on the internet. Every website you visit, every email you send, every activity you participate in (even chat rooms) can all be tracked with your IP address. Remember this the next time you or someone you know thinks of acting out online, because they are "anonymous". To put it simply, you are not anonymous, but instead easily traceable. And if you choose to break laws or violate the rights of others on the internet, you will be caught; Just as others will if they choose to do the same.

Cyber Bullies

Taking the school ground to a new level

CYBER BULLIES

Cyber bullies are, quite simply, people who bully others over the internet. They may send their messages using email, text messages, instant messenger, chat rooms, blogs, or even building entire websites designed to insult or threaten someone.

Unfortunately, cyber bullying usually goes farther than name calling. Cyber bullies are rude and mean to others on the internet because they feel they cannot be caught. If they can't be caught, they can do whatever they want. This creates a dangerous environment, where violence and hate run free.

Some examples of cyber bullying you might see include threats, gossip, hate mail, and even entire websites dedicated to blackmailing people. What makes cyber bullying even more dangerous is that it is often unseen by adults. Normally, when someone gets bullied, a teacher or a parent will notice and intervene before things get out of hand. However, if the bullying is limited to instant messages, email, text messages and forum posts, parents and other responsible adults likely will not have access to them. It won't even be obvious what is happening until too late. You make take it for granted, but having responsible adults around to intervene is very important. It prevents things from escalating to a level that you and everyone else your age simply cannot handle alone.

There are some very simple ways to avoid cyber bullies. First, ignore them! Remember that the best thing about the internet is that YOU control what you want to see and read. If you don't want to see or read something a cyber bully is saying to you, ignore them. Cyber bullies enjoy this activity because they get a reaction from people. If you don't give a reaction, they won't have a reason to bother you. The "close" button works wonders for this.

There are warning signs that friends or parents may be the victim of cyber bullying. Watch for these signs, and if you suspect they are being victimized, get help for them immediately! Often victims of cyber bullying will be unwilling or even afraid to seek help themselves. The only way to help them is to get help for them.

Cyber bullying is actually one of the easiest of internet crimes to detect. Victims of cyber bullying may spend long hours on their computer, close windows or shut off the monitor when you come in the room, be secretive about their online activities, suddenly change their behavior, may get mysterious telephone calls during the day or late at night, fear of leaving the house, crying for no obvious reason, low self esteem, unexplained broken or lost possessions or money, and excuses that don't seem to make sense. Essentially, these signs all show feelings of helplessness, fear, suspicion and emotional pain.

If cyber bullying ever begins to involve threats to yourself or others, or to any property, you need to tell a responsible adult right away. Eventually they will find out, and surely you would rather have their help now than have them find out after something bad has happened. Remember, adults aren't there to make you look "geeky", or to "embarrass" you, or to get angry at you. They are there to protect you and keep you as safe as possible. All you have to do is be a responsible young adult and tell them when you need their help.

Adult Content

The birds and the bees, internet style

PORNOGRAPHY

We all see it. It is all over the internet. It is hard to avoid, and often accidental. It is pornography. It makes up 12% of all websites on the internet, 8% of all emails, 35% of all downloads, and 25% of all search engine requests. The average age of first exposure to internet pornography is 11 years old. Eleven! It is easy to see why. The adult industry is worth $57 billion each year to the world's economy. That's $57,000,000,000.00; more than the combined annual revenue of all professional baseball, basketball, football and hockey franchises in North America. That is a large incentive to get internet users hooked, and hooked young.

There are risks involved, such as suspension from school or contracting viruses and Trojans on your computer. However, the most important thing to know about adult content on the internet is what to do when it happens to you.

Statistics show that almost one fifth of all young people accidentally end up on an adult website within a one year period. These aren't the ones who just "say" it was an accident; these are real kids who accidentally stumbled onto the wrong website. It is actually very easy to do. Adult website managers often employ tricky tactics to get users onto their websites. An adult site web master may find a way to install a script on your computer that changes your home page to their website. Changing it back will appear to work, but once you reboot your computer, the site is back again. Some adult websites earn money for every website view they have. They make agreements with other websites to show a "pop-up" or "pop-under" window when you visit the other company's website. Often times there will be a built-in script with the window that causes hundreds of other windows to open every time you close one. Some adult sites purposely mask themselves as other websites. They will often buy up old URLs that once pointed to more friendly content in an attempt to get more traffic to their website. Some websites will even bury certain keywords, like the names of popular toys, in the coding of their website where search engines can find it. Anyone searching for that particular toy can end up at an adult website.

You should also know the warning signs to recognize if a friend or family member is viewing adult content. Remember that viewing these websites intentionally while under the age of majority is a crime. You can help prevent internet crimes by watching for warning signs like friends spending large amounts of time at the computer, clearing the internet history every time they go online, closing windows when you walk in the room, or muting the volume on their computer all the time.

The important thing to know here is that some adult website owners make it very easy for you to accidentally end up on their website. If you happen to end up there by accident, don't just sit and worry that you will get caught. Be proactive, and go tell a responsible adult what happened right away. Chances are, if you go and tell them that you just accidentally ended up at an adult website and didn't know what to do, they will thank you for being honest and help you to avoid it in the future.

Sex, Drugs, And Parental Controls?

WOULD YOU LET HIM DO YOUR HOMEWORK?

Imagine, for a moment, what you picture a "drug user" or "drug addict" to look like. Do you picture a highly intelligent, well presented individual? Or someone who has more fingers than brain cells? If nothing else, you most likely didn't choose the first possibility. Many of the individuals in society who participate in these activities also end up with mental and/or intellectual challenges as a result of their addiction.

Now, think for a moment of someone at school you know who uses drugs. You may not know them personally, but they are in every school. We have all met them, and they are the "Stoners". Imagine you had an important assignment coming due in a week. This homework assignment would mean the difference between an "A+" or a fail in the class, depending on how well you did. It is a sink or swim assignment. Would you ask one of "The Stoners" to do it for you? Would you trust their intelligence and information to pass that class? Or would you do it yourself, knowing you could do better?

Your answer above is very important. If you wouldn't let a stoner write an assignment for school, why would you trust them with your life? Illegal drugs are no joke. Marijuana, ecstasy, methamphetamines, cocaine, heroin and countless other drugs kill thousands of people each and every year. They can be extremely dangerous, and even the tiniest amounts can be lethal. Why would you trust your life to a drug addict?

If you ever think of reading information on drugs from the internet, consider this. Who are the people who know so much about drugs? Who are the people who are willing to share it? Who are the people who have access to this kind of information whenever they want it? Drug addicts do. If you are reading information on the internet about "how to buy drugs" or "how to make drugs" or "getting high at home", you are most likely reading something that was written by a drug addict. Knowing that drugs like these are potentially lethal, and knowing that you wouldn't even trust a simple homework assignment to a stoner, why on earth would you trust them with your life?

You are an intelligent young adult, and you can make the right decisions. It may sound cliché, but you are the future of this world. Without you, there is no future. A world without you is a world without hope. You deserve to live a long and happy life, and the world deserves to have you. Use your head, don't do drugs, and don't rely on the internet to teach you about them. Instead, sit down and talk to your parents.

It may feel uncomfortable at first, but really your parents want you to talk to them about things like this. They have already been through what you are going through; All the peer pressure, the media glorification, everything you are seeing about drugs they have already seen. Your parents are the one group of people on earth who will be honest with you about drugs. They won't talk to you like a child, they won't just say "don't do drugs", like so many after-school specials. Your parents will tell you the truth, answer your questions, and help you through this time. Use that resource to your full advantage.

SEX INFORMATION ON THE INTERNET

One day while surfing the internet, you might find yourself curious about sex. That is a normal part of being a young adult. Sex is something that you are bombarded with each and every day, and yet you likely haven't had any experience with it. It is natural to be curious. But the internet is not the best resource to learn about sex.

Think for a minute about the information you find on the internet about sex. First, you will likely find a lot of pornography. You may even stumble onto illegal websites. This is not the way to go. There are three resources that can help you to find information about sex. One is this book; Another, your school; And of course, your parents can help teach you about sex.

It may seem uncomfortable to talk to your parents about sex, but remember this. Your parents once had "the talk" with their parents, and their parents had "the talk" with their parents. "The talk" is something that every young adult experiences at one point or another. Remember also that your parents now have more information at their fingertips than ever before. They are encouraged by the media, the schools, and other parents to talk to you about sex. They know how to do it right, with as little "uncomfortable silence" as possible. If you have questions about sex, your parents should be your first resource.

Your school also has several resources available to

them to help with your quest for information. Years ago, sex education in schools only taught abstinence. Nowadays, schools teach young adults everything they need to know about sex. From the "mechanics" of the birds and the bees, to Sexually Transmitted Diseases, to pregnancy and beyond. Schools have learned that the "just don't do it" approach doesn't work with intelligent young adults today. So they give reasons why you should abstain from sex, as well as how to be safe if you do engage in those activities. Your school likely has a sexual education teacher, or a counselor who specializes in that information. If you have questions, you can also ask them.

If you are determined to find information about sexuality and your sexual health using the internet, there are ways to find this information while still staying safe. The most important thing is to tell your parents what you are doing. They will likely help point you in the right directions, and you are less likely to get in trouble for visiting those kinds of websites. For starters, you should avoid just typing "sex" into your search engine. The websites that pop up will not be the ones you are looking for. Try visiting sites like www.HowStuffWorks.com, www.Wikipedia.org, or www. KidsHealth.org. These are all websites that are designed to teach you, rather than sell you pornographic material. Ask your parents to direct you to some websites, or ask your school counselor if they have any websites to suggest. The best way to find information about your sexuality online is to ask someone offline to point you in the right direction. Even your local librarian might be able to help.

The Band-Aid Solution

Why parental controls on your computer don't completely protect you.

BEWARE THE JACK-OF-ALL-TRADES

Today it is becoming easier and easier to find software on the internet that claims to protect you from internet crime and websites you, as a young adult, shouldn't be viewing. Do a search engine search for "parental controls", and you will find millions of results. While much of this software is effective in some ways, no one parental control can protect you completely. In fact, they may just be giving you a false sense of security.

Parental controls work by blocking certain kinds of websites on the internet. When you type in a URL in your web browser, the parental control will search the text of the web page. If they find words that may not be suitable for you to view, they will block the web page. However, this is not a catch-all solution. Many websites may not have the right words to trigger a parental control, but still have content that isn't suitable for you to view. Other resources, like chat rooms and instant messengers, are not blocked. This leaves a lot to be desired when it comes to filtering the content you have available to you on the internet.

There are solutions that will do almost the opposite of a typical parental control, and only allow you to view websites that your parents have already approved. The problem with this solution is that it takes a lot of time to set up, and if you find a new website you would like to view – even if it is "ColoringBook.com" or something similar, your parents have to manually review and approve it.

As you can see, there is no one solution that can protect you on the internet completely. However, using a combination of parental controls and your own intelligence, you can stay safe on the internet. While it may seem that parental controls are only there to restrict what you can do on the internet, it is important to remember that they are there for your own personal safety.

If you or your parents are looking for a good software solution, there are a few things to look for. First, you should be able to block websites on demand. You should be able to filter specific content from being viewed, and take screenshots of that content if necessary. The software should automatically record all instant messages, emails, websites, and keystrokes on the computer, and should be accessible from anywhere over the internet, allowing your parents to monitor your activities while they are at work.

One solution has been found that is very highly recommended. It is called WebWatcher, and is available from AwarenessTech at AwarenessTech.com. It has won several awards, including several "Editor's Choice" awards, and has been featured on CNN and CBS, as well as in publications offered by Newsweek and CNet. As well as having all of the recommended features above, it can also monitor several computers at once, monitors in real-time, is completely invisible on the computers that have it installed, it cannot be stopped by anti-spyware, anti-virus or firewall software, and can even monitor different users on the same computer (so you can see who is doing the viewing).

Just remember that using this or any other software will not guarantee your safety on the internet. While it may help protect you, the only thing that can really protect you is your own common sense.

Online Predators

ONLINE PREDATORS

An online predator is essentially an online stalker. They may follow you around online, chat with you constantly, send you disturbing photographs, and insist on meeting with you in person. Online predators are probably the most well known danger on the internet, and they are also the most dangerous. There are several things you should know about online predators, and the way they act.

First, online predators will establish themselves as "one of the group". This means pretending to be just another young adult in the chat room or forum. Predators will typically assume the identity of a teenage girl, because they feel teenage girls connect more easily with other teenage girls. An online predator will introduce themselves, listen to your problems, and try to seem like a really great friend. They will slowly begin to introduce mature content into your conversations, as a way of testing the waters. They may even show you pictures or videos of an adult nature. Many predators will use this time to evaluate the possibility of their "prey" meeting them face-to-face. Younger teens are especially at risk. Online predators see them as vulnerable and naive, making them prime targets.

Predators will often take their time luring in their prey, often sending them gifts through the mail and giving them private email accounts and phone numbers to make contact with. Some predators will even register a toll-free number, so that long distance charges won't "tip off" your parents to the crime.

Online predators are stalkers. They are committing harassment, and harassment is a crime punishable by law. If you are a victim of an online predator, you are a victim of harassment. You have the right to justice, and you should seek that justice starting with your local police force. Police take these kinds of complaints very seriously, because they know what can happen if they don't.

There are many ways to avoid this situation all together. Primarily, be responsible in your online activities. Don't use un-moderated chat rooms, as predators will usually hang out there. Moderated chat rooms have the ability to "kick" a user out if they begin disrupting the group and making individuals uncomfortable.

Try to avoid "PMs", or private messages, unless it is someone you have met in person. Using a moderated chat room means nothing in private chat, because no one can monitor what happens there. It is the same as meeting new people in person. You always want to meet in a public place for safety. Online, make sure you meet everyone in a public area. It really will keep you safe.

Don't respond to "PMs" from people you don't know. Often they will seem nice, but as soon as you reply they know they have found their target. It is important to have someone to watch over your interactions with new people for your own safety.

If you ever agree to meet face-to-face with an online friend, there are several things you should do. First, tell a responsible adult where you will be and what you are doing. Ask your parents if they feel it is okay. Second, be sure to meet somewhere that is very public, like the library or coffee shop. Third, and most important, never go alone. Always have at least two friends with you when you meet an online "friend". That way, if they do turn out to be a predator, they will be less likely to attempt to hurt you with someone who is watching you.

It is very important in today's society to watch out for your friends and family. There are specific warning signs associated with victims of cyber stalking, and they should be taken seriously. Often a victim will spend large amounts of time on the computer. They may have pornographic images stored in their "received files" folder. They may send or receive phone calls from people you don't know. Often, victims will receive gifts in the mail, and may become withdrawn from family and friends. This is because a common tactic of online predators is to turn the victim against their family and friends to reduce the risk of the victim reporting the crime.

The most important thing to know about staying safe from online predators is to be responsible, and never be afraid of telling someone you trust. Remember, if an online predator tries to take advantage of you, YOU are the victim. Tell a responsible adult whom you trust. They will be glad you came to them before anything happened.

Spam

Not just for sandwiches anymore

UNSOLICITED COMMERCIAL EMAIL

Unsolicited commercial email, otherwise known as spam, is a large problem on the internet. Some studies have shown that as much as 80% of all email sent online is spam. Although it may be a nuisance, spammers (as they are called) don't just send out this email to annoy. They send out these emails to profit. The Direct Marketing Association did a study in 2004 that showed that spam is worth $11 billion U.S. Approximately 1 in 20 individuals who receive a spam message will reply to it or click the link contained within the message. Even legitimate marketers have a hard time getting that many people to read their email.

THE OTHER RISKS

Unfortunately, email isn't the only way to receive spam. Spam can also be sent by instant messenger, through chat rooms, on forums or blogs, and even in search engines. Spammers will go to great lengths to devise new ways of deceiving people out of their money. If a spammer spends five hours researching a new spam tactic, and then sends out a spam that brings them $1000, they are making $200 an hour. That is a large incentive to innovate in this underground industry.

Spam isn't only scamming individuals out of their money. It is also a growing cause of virus and Trojan infection on computers. While anti-spam software can catch most spam email, it can't possibly catch it all. Often the email that does get through the filters contains harmful viruses that can attack your computer and steal your personal information. The only real way of stopping problems like these on your computer is never to open email from someone you don't know.

TIPS FOR PREVENTING SPAM

There are ways to prevent spam and the risks associated with it. First and most importantly, protect your email address. Posting your email address in a chat room, on a website, or giving it away when signing up for a website are three easy ways to get your email address into the hands of spammers. Look at everything you receive in your inbox with doubt and skepticism. If it sounds too good to be true, it probably is.

Double check "urban legend" type email. This is one of the easiest things to do. If you get a "warning" email about a certain product causing harm or catching fire, chances are you are receiving a hoax. Just to be sure, double check the information on the internet. There are entire websites dedicated to revealing these warnings as false. Try www.Snopes.com to double check your information. You can also create a separate email address for "signing up". This way, when you have to enter your email address to access certain websites or content, you can provide your "throw away" email address. Your real inbox never receives the spam.

Never open attachments unless you requested them. Sometimes, even your friends and family can have their computers infected with viruses. These viruses will often send out an email to everyone in that person's address book with an attachment, usually containing the virus. The safest thing to do is not to open attachments unless you are expecting them. You should never respond in any way to spam. Even clicking the "unsubscribe" link only verifies that your email address is valid, and you end up with even more spam. Never use your "I'm on vacation" auto-reply for the same reason; it will verify to the spammer that your email address does work. Use your spam filters instead. Some spam filters can even be set so high that you have to "white-list" anyone you want to receive email from, and everything else is sent to your junk email folder. This is especially effective because then only people you have given permission to can send you email. You should never respond to any emails asking for your name, password, or any other personal information. Often emails like this will appear to come from reliable sources, such as your bank. Remember that real companies will already have your information, and they would never send you an email requesting it.

The best thing that you can do to stop spam is to simply delete it. If everyone stopped clicking links and buying products from spam, it would no longer be profitable and would simply go away. Be a part of the solution!

Gambling

Poker isn't all fun and games

Online poker has become a growing trend among young people today. Television shows and commercials glorifying online gambling are an every day occurrence. But there is more than meets the eye when it comes to online poker.

Something that may not be obvious is that online gambling, or any form of gambling, is illegal for young adults. Until you reach the age of majority in your state or province, online gambling is punishable by law. There is a reason for this. Gambling is a problem for many individuals in society. It can destroy lives, consuming all of your time and money. It can destroy your credit rating if you use credit cards to pay for your habit. It is important to remember that online casinos are in business to make a profit. They profit by taking in more than they pay out. Most of the time, the occasional win is offset by large losses.

Something that is becoming increasingly important is the use of credit cards for online gambling. If you use your own credit card, you could ruin your credit rating. This can make it harder or even impossible for you to buy a house, a car, or even keep you from working in some industries. If you use your parents' credit card, not only can you get grounded and punished, but using someone else's credit card is technically identity theft and fraud. It is punishable by law, and may involve serious fines, a criminal record, or even jail time. Fraud charges are outside of your parents' control, meaning they cannot choose not to "press charges". If you get caught committing fraud, even using your parents' information, you will be charged.

Online gambling can become addictive very easily. It is easy to be lured in by the promise of instant riches, only a mouse click away. You can quickly forget about the hundreds or even thousands of dollars you put into your gambling habit on your way to those so-called millions.

There are some ways to avoid the risks of online gambling. You should ignore advertisements for online gaming websites. They are not intended for you. Avoid gambling websites all together. Advertisers intentionally like to make their websites appealing to you once you arrive, practically screaming at you to take out your credit card. If you arrive at one accidentally, click away immediately. Advertisers will often attempt to lure you with offers of free money to play with. Don't fall for it! This money is only available once you make a large deposit, usually over $100.

Try to avoid sites that offer gambling without real money. Gambling of any kind creates a pattern, which is what these websites intend. Once you start gambling, it is even easier to make the transition to betting real money. Remember that gambling is illegal for minors. If you were to win anything, these websites will go to great lengths to verify your age. If you are a minor, you don't get your winnings. For young people, online gambling isn't a game of chance – it's a guaranteed loss.

The safest bet you can make online is that internet gambling will not be beneficial to you. So stay safe, and stay away. Don't bet online; you could be gambling with more than just your money.

Internet Addiction

It is not an urban myth

Internet addiction is a growing problem among young people. With easy access to all varieties of entertainment only a click away, young people are finding it easier and easier to isolate them. Internet addiction has now become widely recognized as a disorder. Although some do not classify it as an addiction, over-use of the internet is still a cause for concern no matter who you ask.

There are more risks involved in internet addiction than you may think, many leading to permanent physical ailments. You can develop Carpal Tunnel Syndrome, a debilitating joint problem in the hands and wrists. This is caused by the posture you sit in while at your computer, and the repetitive movements involved in typing. Carpal Tunnel Syndrome can prevent you from most major types of office work in the future, limiting your career possibilities. Spending too much time on the computer can also cause dry eyes, leading to blurred vision. If you wear contacts, this can be even more serious; dry eyes can lead to bacterial infections that can potentially cause blindness.

Migraine headaches are a permanent effect of internet addiction, as many sufferers will have migraines their entire lives after the first occurrence. Backaches can develop from improper posture. This can lead to severe pain later in life, severely limiting your abilities to cope with daily living as early as your 30's and 40's. Skipping meals is common among internet addicts, and this can lead to eating disorders. Many internet addicts are overweight because of a combination of factors, primarily abnormal eating habits and lack of activity.

Lack of personal hygiene can become a problem for internet addicts, as the online world doesn't "care" if you don't shower. However, this can cause more problems than just a bad odor. If you neglect brushing your teeth, you risk causing cavities and tooth decay, as well as setting the stage for an abscess. An abscess in your mouth can cause brain damage similar to that of a serious stroke, and can even be fatal. Sleep patterns will often change for internet addicts, leading to a reduction in ability to focus during important activities such as school and work.

You should be aware of the warning signs for internet addiction. If you see yourself, your friends, or any of your family members exhibiting any of these signs, you need to speak to them or a counselor about their internet usage. Some warning signs are obvious, such as spending time online when you should be doing other things such as homework or chores, sneaking online when no one is around, and being preoccupied with getting "back online" when away from the computer. However, there are several other signs to watch out for.

Internet addicts will often lose track of time while they are online, sacrificing sleep to spend time on their computers. They may become agitated or angry when their time online is interrupted. They will often prefer spending time online rather than being with friends or family. They will disobey internet time limits set by parents, and lie about how much time they really spend online. They may become more tired or irritable than they were before the internet became a part of their life. They will often appear irritable or moody when they don't have access to the computer, but their mood will improve immediately once they log back on. They may even exhibit a completely different personality while on the computer, similar to a drug addict on a high.

Luckily, there are ways to prevent internet addiction. Play sports, go hang out with friends, or even just pick up a book. The internet is not your only source of entertainment, and is not your only social outlet. Choose other options when they are available, and only use the internet as an "extra resource" for homework assignments and the occasional email. Your social life, and your health, will benefit greatly.

If you or someone you know is experiencing an internet addiction, there is help available. Talk to your school counselors, your parents, or even your older siblings. Ironically, there are also many websites dedicated to the topic of internet addiction that may actually help. Just try to avoid becoming addicted to them.

The bottom line with internet addiction is that it is just like any other addiction. Life doesn't seem fulfilling for the addict, so they seek out a way to fill their time and their minds. The internet provides an escape for them. People can become so dependent on this escape that even without chemical dependence, which occurs in most addictions, internet addicts cannot function properly without their daily "fix". Remember that there is a whole big world out there to explore. You don't need to escape from it. If what you are doing isn't fulfilling, go find something else. There is a world of possibilities, and 99% of them are offline!

Part II

Just for Parents

Inside this section

This section has been included in this book for the sole benefit of parents. While this book is targeted towards young teens and pre-teens, parents are obviously the ones who will purchase this book. You have purchased this book for the benefit of your kids, or kids you know. Perhaps you are a parent of a pre-teen who is experiencing problems on the internet. Maybe you are a teacher who wanted some material to use in class. Maybe you are a grandparent who purchased this book for your grandchildren. In any case, this section of the book is dedicated to you.

This section of the book is intended to help prepare you for the contents of the above chapters. It will help you in three key ways; First, it will help prepare you to talk with your kids about this book and why they should read it. It will prepare you for discussions you may have as a result. Second, these chapters will show you what you need to protect your children from, which is the basis of this book. Finally, these chapters will give you tips on what to watch out for in your children's behavior, and prevention & action steps you can take to protect your kids.

So, without further adieu, the following two chapters are for you.

The Hard Part

In a perfect world, kids could go online freely. They would never have to worry about pornography, online gambling, abductions or predators. There would be no worry about the latest virus, no phishing attacks, no spyware, adware, or malware. In a perfect world, you could put a computer in your child's room for homework purposes without worrying about sexual predators taking them away. You could let your child chat with friends on the internet and know that their friends were real kids, not perverts pretending to be.

The sad fact is, we don't live in a perfect world, and every one of those things above is something to worry about. That is why it is important to talk to your kids about internet safety. There are other reasons to talk to your kids about safety as well.

First, you want to approach your kids about internet risks before they are exposed to them. Remember when you were a kid, and you did something you thought was bad? Did you run to tell your parents, hoping you wouldn't get in trouble? Of course not, you kept it to yourself. And that is what you need to prevent, by getting to your kids before the internet does. If you talk openly and honestly about the dangers on the internet, your kids will know that it is a topic you feel comfortable discussing. They will be much more likely to come and discuss it with you when they have a problem.

Second, you want your kids to know how to be aware of a bad situation long before they end up in one. This is a lot like why we tell our kids to look both ways before crossing the street. We want them to know how to avoid getting hit by a car without having to actually get hit to learn. It may feel uncomfortable now, but imagine talking to little Suzy or Johnnie after they get rescued from an online predator. THAT conversation would be uncomfortable.

You really want to talk to your kids before they get exposed to online dangers so that they know you can talk about it. There are several reasons in the mind of a child not to come running when they are in trouble. They might be afraid of getting in trouble, or losing their computer privileges. They may be embarrassed at the situation, or not want to disappoint you. They may think you will over react, ground them, punish them, or even hate them. They could even be convinced by an online predator that you cannot be trusted.

If it is so important to talk to your kids about online safety, how do you do it? It isn't easy, but there are a few ways to make the situation more comfortable for both of you. Timing of these conversations is very important. You want to do this as naturally as possible, so your kids don't think you have planned the whole conversation (even if you have). If you have more than one child, it is best to have these conversations separately to give age appropriate information to each child. Sometimes, the best place for uncomfortable conversation is in the car. It is completely private, there are no interruptions, and during the really uncomfortable parts you don't have to look your kids in the eye. Of course you should be careful and still give plenty of attention to the road.

There are some easy ways to "lead in" to the conversation. Try thinking of a topic on TV or in the movies that is related. Try something you saw in a tabloid headline after leaving the grocery store together. Or, you can just come out with it and ask if they have ever seen pornography online. Ask them if they use blogs or instant messengers. These are all important things to know, no matter how hard they may be to ask.

The most important thing is to remember to talk with your kids, and not just to your kids. Conversation is a two-way street, which means you both have to speak. Asking probing questions, such as "how do you feel about this?" or "what do you think?" can help break the ice if they aren't willing to speak. If they are going to feel comfortable coming to you when they really need you, they need to know that you will be talking with them and not lecturing them. Lectures have a time and a place, and internet education just isn't one of them.

It is also important to let them know why you are talking to them about this, and why you care. You obviously don't want to see them hurt, so tell them that. Don't be afraid to be honest during this conversation either. If you don't know the answer to something, say so. Maybe you can figure it out together, so you can both learn new things. Remember, the more often you discuss topics like this, the easier it will become.

The topics you should cover with your kids have, in large part, been covered in this book. That is why this book will be an excellent resource for you. This book is written in such a way that, if you choose, you can read these chapters yourself first. Then, sit down with your kids and read the remaining chapters together. It will help guide you through to conversation, from why they need to know about internet safety to how they can protect their friends using their new-found knowledge.

What To Watch For

It is important for you to know what dangers there are on the internet and how to recognize when your child has become a victim. That is what this section is dedicated to. If just one parent learns how to recognize the signs of an internet crime, then one more child is safe.

Here are some general statistics about kids and the internet. Be aware, some of these are quite shocking.

Internet use is coming earlier and earlier. An astonishing 67 percent of preschool aged children already use computers, and 23 percent of preschoolers use the internet.

14-17 year olds receive the highest percentage of pornographic spam.

94% of kids top 50 favorite websites collect personal information through the use of contests, surveys, and other forms.

27% of kids say that they would give out their real name and address in their instant messenger profile (which you don't have to give permission for someone to view.)

19% of kids say that they have accidentally stumbled onto a pornographic website during the last year.

34% of kids have been bullied, and 27% of those kids have been bullied on the internet.

60% of students pretend to be someone else while they're online.

5% of students reply to the spam they receive in an attempt to stop it.

Spam is estimated to be worth $11 billion to the US economy every year.

57% of grade 4 & 5 students say they do their homework online every day. By grade 11, that number jumps to 91%.

35% of boys in grades 7 to 11 have purposely accessed violent or hateful content on the internet.

28% of kids' top 50 favorite sites contain violent or hateful content.

The statistics just continue on and on like this. It is quite startling to realize what today's kids are exposed to on a daily basis. There are ways to protect them, as will be discussed later in this chapter.

As you can see, there are a few main categories of internet crime to be aware of. Invasions of privacy, pornography, cyber bullying, online predators, spam, misinformation, violent or hateful content, gambling, and internet addiction are all things to be aware of on the internet. Your best weapon against these threats is something you already have: Knowledge.

Here are some common warning signs that your child may be a victim of an internet crime:

Watch for secretive behavior, or spending large amounts of time on the computer. More than a few hours each day likely means that they are engaged in activities they shouldn't be.

Unexplained phone calls or gifts from people you don't know may be a sign that your child is a victim of an online predator, as they often use these tactics on their victims.

Your kids deleting all of the history, temporary files, etc. from the computer when they are finished using it is a sign they are viewing inappropriate websites.

Quickly closing or minimizing windows when you enter a room often means they were viewing something you aren't meant to see.

Strange files appearing on your computer may be viruses, spyware, adware, or malware; They could even be inappropriate photographs sent by online predators.

Kids telling you they are going to meet friends, but not telling you who. This could be a sign that they are meeting an online friend.

Reluctance to leave the computer can be a sign of internet addiction.

Unwillingness to go to school or other social activities that your child is normally enthusiastic about may be a sign of cyber bullying.

Strange charges on your credit card, or possessions going missing may be signs that your child has a problem with internet gambling.

As you can see, there are ways to spot behavioral changes in your kids that warn you of possible inappropriate content or internet crimes. But remember, you are your kids' first line of defense. You control the parental controls on the computer, you control the time they spend on the computer, and where it is located in your home. Only you can take the right steps to protect your kids.

Part III

The Expert Opinion

Internet Safety Resources

Included in this section, are several internet safety resources for you. First, there are short articles/publications offered by the government, non-profit agencies, and other not-for-profit organizations dedicated to helping you stay safe on the internet. Then there are a list of websites you can visit if you need help or advice about internet safety.

Articles & Publications on Internet Safety

THE FBI'S INTERNET SAFETY TIPS

Source: "http://www.fbi.gov/kids/k5th/safety2.htm"

There are some very important things that you need to keep in mind when you're on your computer at home or at school.

First, remember never to give out personal information such as your name, home address, school name, or telephone number in a chat room or on bulletin boards. Also, never send a picture of yourself to someone you chat with on the computer without your parent's permission.

Never write to someone who has made you feel uncomfortable or scared.

Do not meet someone or have them visit you without the permission of your parents.

Tell your parents right away if you read anything on the Internet that makes you feel uncomfortable.

Remember that people online may not be who they say

they are. Someone who says that "she" is a "12-year-old girl" could really be an older man.

THE FBI'S "PARENT'S GUIDE TO INTERNET SAFETY"

Source: "http://www.fbi.gov/publications/pguide/pguidee.htm"

Dear Parent:

Our children are our Nation's most valuable asset. They represent the bright future of our country and hold our hopes for a better Nation. Our children are also the most vulnerable members of society. Protecting our children against the fear of crime and from becoming victims of crime must be a national priority.

Unfortunately the same advances in computer and telecommunication technology that allow our children to reach out to new sources of knowledge and cultural experiences are also leaving them vulnerable to exploitation and harm by computer-sex offenders.

I hope that this pamphlet helps you to begin to understand the complexities of on-line child exploitation. For further information, please contact your local FBI office or the National Center for Missing and Exploited Children at 1-800-843-5678.

Louis J. Freeh, Former Director

Federal Bureau of Investigation

INTRODUCTION

While on-line computer exploration opens a world of possibilities for children, expanding their horizons and exposing them to different cultures and ways of life, they can be exposed to dangers as they hit the road exploring the information highway. There are individuals who attempt to sexually exploit children through the use of on-line services and the Internet. Some of these individuals gradually seduce their targets through the use of attention, affection, kindness, and even gifts. These individuals are often willing to devote considerable amounts of time, money, and energy in this process. They listen to and empathize with the problems of children. They will be aware of the latest music, hobbies, and interests of children. These individuals attempt to gradually lower children's inhibitions by slowly introducing sexual context and content into their conversations.

There are other individuals, however, who immediately engage in sexually explicit conversation with children. Some offenders primarily collect and trade child-pornographic images, while others seek face-to-face meetings with children via on-line contacts. It is important for parents to understand that children can be indirectly victimized through conversation, i.e. "chat," as well as the transfer of sexually explicit information and material. Computer-sex offenders may also be evaluating children they come in contact with on-line for future face-to-face contact and direct victimization. Parents and children should remember that a computer-sex offender can be any age or sex the person does not have to fit the caricature of a dirty, unkempt, older man wearing a raincoat to be someone who could harm a child.

Children, especially adolescents, are sometimes interested in and curious about sexuality and sexually explicit material. They may be moving away from the total control of parents and seeking to establish new relationships outside their family. Because they may be curious, children/adolescents sometimes use their on-line access to actively seek out such materials and individuals. Sex offenders targeting children will use and exploit these characteristics and needs.

Some adolescent children may also be attracted to and lured by on-line offenders closer to their age who, although not technically child molesters, may be dangerous. Nevertheless, they have been seduced and manipulated by a clever offender and do not fully understand or recognize the potential danger of these contacts.

This guide was prepared from actual investigations involving child victims, as well as investigations where law enforcement officers posed as children. Further information on protecting your child on-line may be found in the National Center for Missing and Exploited Children's Child Safety on the Information Highway and Teen Safety on the Information Highway pamphlets.

WHAT ARE SIGNS THAT YOUR CHILD MIGHT BE AT RISK ON-LINE?

Your child spends large amounts of time on-line, especially at night.

Most children that fall victim to computer-sex offenders spend large amounts of time on-line, particularly in chat rooms. They may go on-line after dinner and on the weekends. They may be latchkey kids whose parents have told them to stay at home after school. They go on-line to chat with friends, make new friends, pass time, and sometimes look for sexually explicit information. While much of the knowledge and experience gained may be valuable, parents should consider monitoring the amount of time spent on-line.

Children on-line are at the greatest risk during the evening hours. While offenders are on-line around the clock, most work during the day and spend their evenings on-line trying to locate and lure children or seeking pornography.

You find pornography on your child's computer.

Pornography is often used in the sexual victimization of children. Sex offenders often supply their potential victims with pornography as a means of opening sexual discussions and for seduction. Child pornography may be used to show the child victim that sex between children and adults is "normal." Parents should be conscious of the fact that a child may hide the pornographic files on diskettes from them. This may be especially true if the computer is used by other family members.

Your child receives phone calls from men you don't know or is making calls, sometimes long distance, to numbers you don't recognize.

While talking to a child victim on-line is a thrill for a computer-sex offender, it can be very cumbersome. Most want to talk to the children on the telephone. They often engage in "phone sex" with the children and often seek to set up an actual meeting for real sex.

While a child may be hesitant to give out his/her home phone number, the computer-sex offenders will give out theirs. With Caller ID, they can readily find out the child's phone number. Some computer-sex offenders have even obtained toll-free 800 numbers, so that their potential victims can call them without their parents finding out. Others will tell the child to call collect. Both of these methods result in the computer-sex offender being able to find out the child's phone number.

Your child receives mail, gifts, or packages from someone you don't know.

As part of the seduction process, it is common for offenders to send letters, photographs, and all manner of gifts to their potential victims. Computer-sex offenders have even sent plane tickets in order for the child to travel across the country to meet them.

Your child turns the computer monitor off or quickly changes the screen on the monitor when you come into the room.

A child looking at pornographic images or having sexually explicit conversations does not want you to see it on the screen.

Your child becomes withdrawn from the family.

Computer-sex offenders will work very hard at driving a wedge between a child and their family or at exploiting their relationship. They will accentuate any minor problems at home that the child might have. Children may also become withdrawn after sexual victimization.

Your child is using an on-line account belonging to someone else.

Even if you don't subscribe to an on-line service or Internet service, your child may meet an offender while on-line at a friend's house or the library. Most computers come pre-loaded with on-line and/or Internet software. Computer-sex offenders will sometimes provide potential victims with a computer account for communications with them.

WHAT SHOULD YOU DO IF YOU SUSPECT YOUR CHILD IS COMMUNICATING WITH A SEXUAL PREDATOR ON-LINE?

Consider talking openly with your child about your suspicions. Tell them about the dangers of computer-sex offenders.

Review what is on your child's computer. If you don't know how, ask a friend, coworker, relative, or other knowledgeable person. Pornography or any kind of sexual communication can be a warning sign.

Use the Caller ID service to determine who is calling your child. Most telephone companies that offer Caller ID also offer a service that allows you to block your number from appearing on someone else's Caller ID. Telephone companies also offer an additional service feature that rejects incoming calls that you block. This rejection feature prevents computer-sex offenders or anyone else from calling your home anonymously.

Devices can be purchased that show telephone numbers that have been dialed from your home phone. Additionally, the last number called from your home phone can be retrieved provided that the telephone is equipped with a redial feature. You will also need a telephone pager to complete this retrieval.

This is done using a numeric-display pager and another phone that is on the same line as the first phone with the redial feature. Using the two phones and the pager, a call is placed from the second phone to the pager. When the paging terminal beeps for you to enter a telephone number, you press the redial button on the first (or suspect) phone. The last number called from that phone will then be displayed on the pager.

Monitor your child's access to all types of live electronic communications (i.e., chat rooms, instant messages, Internet Relay Chat, etc.), and monitor your child's e-mail. Computer-sex offenders almost always meet potential victims via chat rooms. After meeting a child on-line, they will continue to communicate electronically often via e-mail.

Should any of the following situations arise in your household, via the Internet or on-line service, you should immediately contact your local or state law enforcement agency, the FBI, and the National Center for Missing and Exploited Children:

- Your child or anyone in the household has received child pornography;

- Your child has been sexually solicited by someone who knows that your child is under 18 years of age;

- Your child has received sexually explicit images from someone that knows your child is under the age of 18.

If one of these scenarios occurs, keep the computer turned off in order to preserve any evidence for future law enforcement use. Unless directed to do so by the law enforcement agency, you should not attempt to copy any of the images and/or text found on the computer.

WHAT CAN YOU DO TO MINIMIZE THE CHANCES OF AN ON-LINE EXPLOITER VICTIMIZING YOUR CHILD?

Communicate, and talk to your child about sexual victimization and potential on-line danger.

Spend time with your children on-line. Have them teach you about their favorite on-line destinations.

Keep the computer in a common room in the house, not in your child's bedroom. It is much more difficult for a computer-sex offender to communicate with a child when the computer screen is visible to a parent or another member of the household.

Utilize parental controls provided by your service provider and/or blocking software. While electronic chat can be a great place for children to make new friends and discuss various topics of interest, it is also prowled by computer-sex offenders. Use of chat rooms, in particular, should be heavily monitored. While parents should utilize these mechanisms, they should not totally rely on them.

Always maintain access to your child's on-line account and randomly check his/her e-mail. Be aware that your child could be contacted through the U.S. Mail. Be up front with your child about your access and reasons why.

Teach your child the responsible use of the resources on-line. There is much more to the on-line experience than chat rooms.

Find out what computer safeguards are utilized by your child's school, the public library, and at the homes of your child's friends. These are all places, outside your normal supervision, where your child could encounter an on-line predator.

Understand, even if your child was a willing participant in any form of sexual exploitation, that he/she is not at fault and is the victim. The offender always bears the complete responsibility for his or her actions.

Instruct your children:

- to never arrange a face-to-face meeting with someone they met on- line;

- to never upload (post) pictures of themselves onto

the Internet or on-line service to people they do not personally know;

- to never give out identifying information such as their name, home address, school name, or telephone number;

- to never download pictures from an unknown source, as there is a good chance there could be sexually explicit images;

- to never respond to messages or bulletin board postings that are suggestive, obscene, belligerent, or harassing;

- that whatever they are told on-line may or may not be true.

FREQUENTLY ASKED QUESTIONS:

My child has received an e-mail advertising for a pornographic website, what should I do?

Generally, advertising for an adult, pornographic website that is sent to an e-mail address does not violate federal law or the current laws of most states. In some states it may be a violation of law if the sender knows the recipient is under the age of 18. Such advertising can be reported to your service provider and, if known, the service provider of the originator. It can also be reported to your state and federal legislators, so they can be made aware of the extent of the problem.

Is any service safer than the others?

Sex offenders have contacted children via most of the major

on-line services and the Internet. The most important factors in keeping your child safe on-line are the utilization of appropriate blocking software and/or parental controls, along with open, honest discussions with your child, monitoring his/her on-line activity, and following the tips in this pamphlet.

Should I just forbid my child from going on-line?

There are dangers in every part of our society. By educating your children to these dangers and taking appropriate steps to protect them, they can benefit from the wealth of information now available on-line.

HELPFUL DEFINITIONS:

Internet - An immense, global network that connects computers via telephone lines and/or fiber networks to storehouses of electronic information. With only a computer, a modem, a telephone line and a service provider, people from all over the world can communicate and share information with little more than a few keystrokes.

Bulletin Board Systems (BBSs) - Electronic networks of computers that are connected by a central computer setup and operated by a system administrator or operator and are distinguishable from the Internet by their "dial-up" accessibility. BBS users link their individual computers to the central BBS computer by a modem which allows them to post messages, read messages left by others, trade information, or hold direct conversations. Access to a BBS can, and often is, privileged and limited to those users who have access privileges granted by the systems operator.

Commercial On-line Service (COS) - Examples of COSs are America Online, Prodigy, CompuServe and Microsoft

Network, which provide access to their service for a fee. COSs generally offer limited access to the Internet as part of their total service package.

Internet Service Provider (ISP) - Examples of ISPs are Erols, Concentric and Netcom. These services offer direct, full access to the Internet at a flat, monthly rate and often provide electronic-mail service for their customers. ISPs often provide space on their servers for their customers to maintain World Wide Web (WWW) sites. Not all ISPs are commercial enterprises. Educational, governmental and nonprofit organizations also provide Internet access to their members.

Public Chat Rooms - Created, maintained, listed and monitored by the COS and other public domain systems such as Internet Relay Chat. A number of customers can be in the public chat rooms at any given time, which are monitored for illegal activity and even appropriate language by systems operators (SYSOP). Some public chat rooms are monitored more frequently than others, depending on the COS and the type of chat room. Violators can be reported to the administrators of the system (at America On-line they are referred to as terms of service [TOS]) which can revoke user privileges. The public chat rooms usually cover a broad range of topics such as entertainment, sports, game rooms, children only, etc.

Electronic Mail (E-Mail) - A function of BBSs, COSs and ISPs which provides for the transmission of messages and files between computers over a communications network similar to mailing a letter via the postal service. E-mail is stored on a server, where it will remain until the addressee retrieves it. Anonymity can be maintained by the sender by predetermining what the receiver will see as the "from" address. Another way to conceal one's identity is to use an "anonymous remailer," which is a service that allows the user to send an e-mail message repackaged under the remailer's own header, stripping off the originator's name completely.

Chat - Real-time text conversation between users in a chat room with no expectation of privacy. All chat conversation is accessible by all individuals in the chat room while the conversation is taking place.

Instant Messages - Private, real-time text conversation between two users in a chat room.

Internet Relay Chat (IRC) - Real-time text conversation similar to public and/or private chat rooms on COS.

Usenet (Newsgroups) - Like a giant, cork bulletin board where users post messages and information. Each posting is like an open letter and is capable of having attachments, such as graphic image files (GIFs). Anyone accessing the newsgroup can read the postings, take copies of posted items, or post responses. Each newsgroup can hold thousands of postings. Currently, there are over 29,000 public newsgroups and that number is growing daily. Newsgroups are both public and/or private. There is no listing of private newsgroups. A user of private newsgroups has to be invited into the newsgroup and be provided with the newsgroup's address.

Internet Safety for Kids

By Debra Warwick

Now more than ever our children are using the internet for everyday activities such as homework, researching, and even chatting with friends. Children are more comfortable using computers because they have grown up around them.

Children also have an inherent need to freely explore, and the internet is the perfect way for them to do so easily from their own home. This leaves them open to become easy targets for manipulative adults with varying motivations. Some online criminals would rather gain access to personal bank accounts, or steal your identity. Others may try to meet your child in real life to try to sexually or physically assault your child.

The internet provides no more safety than meeting a stranger in real life. Because of the false security, many people get scammed for information and they don't even realize. Many parents and teens alike might not want to believe this, but we should consider the facts. One in five children were solicited online in the past year. One in five were exposed to photos or videos of people with graphic sexual content. Things of this nature are also free and easy for a child to download. The numbers themselves are enough to scare anyone, but situations like this are easier to avoid than you might think!

It's important to talk with your children. Let them know what kind of people could be lurking, no matter how nice they might seem. Instruct your kids to limit online conversation to people you already know. If you have a child that wants to "chat" (strongly suggest otherwise), but if they MUST make sure they know what is appropriate conversation.

Never under any circumstance should your child be allowed to give out any personal information such as name, phone number, email, and especially where they live, work, or go to school. Explain to your children disobeying these safety precautions could seriously harm the financial and physical well being of the entire family.

Parents want to think that our teenagers are older and wiser than our pre teens, but in reality they are more likely to get into trouble on the internet. Teens are more likely to venture around websites, exploring limitless information on everything from their favorite singer to downloading movies.

Teenagers are more curious and will take bigger risks than children. They are also more likely to reach out and chat with people from the internet that they don't know personally. Remind your children that people can pretend to be anyone through a computer, so even if they think they know this person, be careful.

You should have your computer in an area like your living room, so you can monitor your child's actions. To be extra safe you can install monitoring, or download free blocking software that restricts the websites your children can view. Let your children know that you will be monitoring their activity for safety precaution.

Debra, a computer expert, spends her time editing, and runs www.FreeFixIt.net

Internet Safety:
The Missing Link

By Dorothy M. Neddermeyer, PhD

May 22, 2006, the 109th Congress 2nd session declared June as Internet Safety Month. Recently, the National Center for Missing and Exploited Children and Cox Communication released a highly disturbing survey of youth between 13 and 17 years old about their use of the Internet.

- 4 percent of the children questioned have had face-to-face meetings with people they met on the Internet. Even one teen meeting a stranger is one too many.

- 30 percent said they have considered meeting someone face-to-face who they know only through the Internet.

- 71 percent reported receiving messages online from someone they didn't know.

- 45 percent said they have been asked for personal information.

Children have a false sense of safety on the Internet these survey authors posit. It is a common belief among teens that if they use a chat room nickname, people they chat with won't know who they are. This is not true. It is easy to find a person's name, address, school and personal data from the nickname. However, a false sense of safety on the Internet isn't the real issue as to why a teen would be willing to chat with a stranger on the Internet and in 4% of the cases meet the Internet stranger. A child who develops a connection with an adult on the Internet is seeking something which is missing in his/her life.

For example: A child who is painfully shy and fears meeting new people. Whenever it is time for recess, s/he goes off on his/her own, and does not play with the other children. Thus, she/he avoids having to talk to anyone new, and consequently avoids the anxiety associated with new encounters. Child predators know the perfect questions to ask or statements to make to a would-be target to determine if the teen is a child who is seeking something which is missing in their life. They offer love, excitement, physical, emotional, and material comfort, and the means to escape from reality. These can all be rewards. If a child wants these rewards and learns that the Internet 'friend' (predator) will allow him/her to escape, or receive love, or have a lot of fun, she/he will probably turn to the Internet the next time she/he feels these needs. This becomes reinforcing, and the cycle continues.

The list of tips for parents to protect their child on the Internet implies a predator could reach through the Computer screen and pull the child into an abyss. These tips include:

- Create house rules. Create simple, easy-to-read house rules about using the Internet and post them on or near the monitor. Enforce these rules.

- Consider security software for your computers.

- Create passwords. Put Internet accounts in the

parent's name, controlling passwords and using blocking and/or filtering devices.

- Don't be afraid to ask your children to show you their favorite web site and chat rooms. Know with whom your children are exchanging e-mails and chatting.

- Understand the lingo. Instant messaging has its own language.

- Stay alert for warning signs. Be suspicious if your child minimizes the screen when you walk into the room. Be alert to any indication that your child does not want you to know what's going on online. http: www/azag.gov/childrenspage/index.html

The best tip to protect your child from any would-be child Internet predator is to provide them with the love, nurturing, guidance, connectedness and time they need to thrive in life. The guidance they need regarding Internet conversations, no matter the web site is the same as when a stranger calls on the phone or rings the doorbell.

- Never tell a stranger on the Internet any personal information—the same as NEVER telling anyone on the phone that they are home alone or reveal any identifying information.

- Never trust a stranger on the Internet no matter how kind or friendly they seem to be—or if they tell you, "I know your Mom/Dad."

- Never meet an Internet friend (stranger)—the same as NEVER opening the door to a stranger.

Dorothy M. Neddermeyer, PhD, author, "If I'd Only Known...Sexual Abuse in or Out of the Family: A Guide to

Prevention, specializes in Physical/Sexual Abuse Prevention and Recovery. As an inspirational leader, Dr. Neddermeyer empowers people to view life's challenges as an opportunity for Personal/Professional Growth and Spiritual Awakening. http://www.drdorothy.net

Protecting Kids Online

By Pamela Stevens

Careless Internet wandering, by adult or child, is dangerous. The news is full of stories about people who meet online and then have real life encounters with scary or deadly results. This is an extreme situation, most kids are cautious enough to know they should not meet with strangers. Nevertheless, there are other dangers such as your kids being exposed to explicit pornography, violent images or gore, extremist web pages, sexual solicitation, identify theft, malicious content or just simply distraction from what they should be doing, like homework.

Certainly, the Internet is a great resource that puts volumes of valuable knowledge at our fingertips. The Internet helps keep friends and family in touch and provides entertainment and education. Everyday more information and services are going online, so web safety is a subject parents must address.

DANGERS

In order to better formulate Internet guidelines for your children, you need to know the dangers. Here are a few hazards to think about before you talk with your kids.

Pornography

Pornography is easily available online, not only through paid sources but also through pop–ups, unsolicited email, file sharing and search engines. Many sites are landed on accidentally, through misspelled search words or expired domain names. If parents visit these sites, cookies, temporary Internet files or other data is saved onto the computer, which makes it even easier for kids to reach these sites. Teens and preteens may even seek out these sites out of curiosity and end up viewing explicit and sometimes degrading or violent sexual images or video.

Solicitation

Through chat, newsgroups, MySpace, forums, games or email, minors are often approached for sexual contact, nude pictures, web cam video or sexually explicit conversations. Just visit nearly any open chat conversation and you will soon be solicited or asked sexual questions. This even occurs in supposedly kid–friendly rooms.

Predation

Sexual predators may seek out possible sexual contact or exploitation through the Internet. Often they create a user profile that hides who they really are and instigate casual chat conversations to gain the kid's trust. They gradually begin the process of isolating the child, manipulating their self–esteem, enticing them to challenge their boundaries and slowly increase their conversations to sexual topics. They often share pornographic material and may even send things to the child's home.

Violence/Abuse

Anything can be found online, including violent images,

images of corpses, physical abuse, war scenes, executions, animal cruelty, criminal or gang activity and rape. It is unfortunate that people want to share these types of images with the world, but they are out there, and it is a dangerous avenue for your children to explore.

Harassment

Sometimes kids are harassed or intimidated online from people they know or through online games. These types of game bullies are often called griefers.

Extremist Pages

As mentioned, everything is online, including extremist and hate based groups. This includes groups that target gender, minorities, sexual preference, religious or cultural groups and so on. These sites often encourage hate, violence or harassment and may contain derogatory references, cartoon depictions, violent images or harsh language often not filtered out by filtering software.

Computer Viruses, Adware, Spyware

These are harmful to your computer and can be delivered unknowingly through emails, pop–up ads, screen savers or other downloads. If kids are not taught to be Internet savvy, they may download a fun, harmless looking game that sneaks in malicious content to your hard drive. These tiny programs may relate your personal information, monitor how you use the Internet or actually cause damage to your system.

Identity Theft

Kid's identity can be stolen and used. Additionally, if your hard drive is accessed, your information can be stolen, shared and used.

Distraction

Beyond all the real dangers of the Internet, there is simply distraction. Often kids use the computer with the pretense of doing homework, when in reality they are doing their homework, having multiple chat conversations, surfing the net, playing a game, and listening to and downloading music all at the same time. You can easily see why it is hard to get kids to finish their homework and actually learn something when they are dividing their time and attention by so many different things.

PARENT GUIDELINES

Open communication is extremely important. The real dangers of the Internet need to be discussed and your child's possible frustration and resistance to these conversations may need to be addressed as well. Open dialogue is necessary and despite your fear or aggravation, your desire to express your anger should not extend to the point that your child is afraid to talk to you if something does happen.

Setting Boundaries

You and your children, after discussing the dangers and benefits of the Internet, should set some clear boundaries. Keep in mind that boundaries may differ depending on the age of the child, their level of maturity and their willingness to communicate uncomfortable subjects with you. If your child is unenthusiastic about having open conversations with you, they are certainly less likely to talk you if something happens to them online.

Beyond family or individual rules, there are some general guidelines for all Internet users:

Never give out personal information, including name, address, school or employment, telephone or cell number, personal email address or pictures to someone you do not know personally.

Never respond to solicitations or comments that make you uncomfortable.

Never make arrangements to meet someone you have met online. Adults who want to meet people they have met online, should arrange to meet in a public place and with current friends.

Never believe everything you read in a profile, on a message board or in a chat. Often, people pretend or role–play, either for entertainment, to hide or for other ulterior motives.

Never submit your personal information or credit card data to an unsecured site.

Outside of the general guidelines, there are other things to consider for your children, such as:

How long, when and under what circumstances can your children use the Internet?

What sites are they allowed to visit?

What content is off limits?

What kind of communication is allowed, e–mail, chat, IM, etc?

What are your kid's privacy rights?

What should your child do if they experience something that makes them uncomfortable?

What happens if the rules are violated?

After you have established some well–understood guidelines, you should still monitor your kid's Internet activity. Although it is normal for kids to get into a little mischief, such as chatting with their friends when they are supposed to be doing homework, they could also be getting into real trouble. Here are a few warning signs that your kid could be getting into a real dilemma:

Excessive Internet Use

You find pornography or explicit material on their computer

Your child receives mysterious phone calls, emails or text messages

Your child receives mail or gifts from someone you don't know

They are withdrawn, anti–social or avoid talking with you

Your kid quickly changes the screen when you come in the room

You child uses an Internet account that is not their own

They cannot or will not tell you about their online acquaintances

They cut school to get online or sneak on in the middle of the night

Keep in mind, that even if your kid is a willing participant in an exploitive situation, they are still a minor and the victim in the situation. Teens have been known to post provocative images of themselves or initiate explicit conversations, so it is important to keep conversations open and watch for self–esteem, anger or behavioral issues that could be expressed in dangerous ways.

What if exploitation or a child pornography situation occurs?

Unfortunately, odds are your child and even you will be approached online. However, if your kids know how to deal with these situations, it should not escalate into anything. In terms of the law, the following things should be reported:

your child has been sexually solicited by someone who knows that the child is under the age of 18

your child has received sexually explicit images from someone who knows the child is under the age of 18

your child or anyone in the household has received child pornography

If any of the above occur, do not erase anything on your computer and contact your local law enforcement or CyberTipline at www.missingkids.com (1–800–843–5678). If your child has been engaging in a cyber relationship, it is a good idea to seek outside help. Family and teen counselors cannot only help you address the occurrence but also esteem issues that may have attributed to the child's need to seek such a relationship.

CONTROL DEVICES

Fortunately, there is some excellent and helpful software available to help make monitoring kids online activities a little easier. Nothing can replace caring parenting and open communication, but a little extra help is always nice. Here are some software options for parents:

Parental Time Control Software

This software can help parents regulate how much time a kid can spend on the computer and what programs they can access. Most programs allow parents to set specific time limits for time spent online, playing their games or accessing their email or chat. You can also regulate times that you are not home or late at night. Many programs also enable parents to block inappropriate websites and certain keyword searches and lock down the control panel so kids can't make system changes.

Filtering Software

Filtering programs actually block content, websites, pop–ups, explicit images, chats, newsgroups, file sharing and more. Keep in mind that it cannot catch everything, so guidelines still need to be established. Many programs will let you set an approved list of applications, so a child can have access to homework applications like Word, Excel, Microsoft Student and approved websites, without allowing free use of the Internet.

Monitoring Software

Monitoring is a bit different from filtering. Generally monitoring software logs activity as opposed to blocking content. Many offer remote access, so you can receive, through email, a log of your kids' online activities and approve or disprove the sites they are trying to visit or files they want to download. Monitoring programs can save screen shots as well as keystrokes and passwords. Most sources agree that you should tell your kids that you are monitoring their activity, so it is not a secret that could cause conflict later.

Parents

The best software, although a great assistant, cannot replace good parenting. Get to know your kids' Internet preferences, the sites they visit and games they play. Know and manage their email accounts, visit their MySpace pages often and keep track of their user names. Be leery of online friends. Talk to them, become familiar with their favorite websites and discuss your concerns over content and safety. Free, unmonitored Internet use and downloading is never a good idea. Set firm, understood rules and install some good programs to back up your regulations. Always keep your kid's computer out in the open and with a big monitor to make it hard to hide content and keep kids from trying to sneak around in sites they shouldn't or spending all their time chatting instead of doing homework. Block computer use during late night hours and when you are not home. Peak over their shoulder often and talk to them about controversial material, what is in the news, jokes they see, words or phrases they do not understand.

There are many subjects to think about and discuss with your children, the Internet is an unlimited, invaluable source of knowledge, communication and entertainment but should be constrained by acknowledged guidelines, caution and helpful control programs.

References

(2000, April). Online monitoring . Retrieved April 24, 2006, from Smart Computing Web site: http://www.smartcomputing.com/editorial/article.asp?article=articles/archive/g0804/49g04/49g04.asp&guid=

(2004, Dec 14). Kids and the internet. Frequently asked questions. Retrieved Apr 24, 2006, from Microsoft Web site: http://www.microsoft.com/athome/security/children/kidsafetyfaq.mspx

(2006,Mar 27). The Multitasking Generation. Retrieved Apr 24, 2006, from TIME–Archive Web site: http://www.time.com/time/archive/preview/0,10987,1174696,00.html

A parent's guide to internet safety. Retrieved April 24, 2006, from Federal Bureau of Investigation Web site: http://www.fbi.gov/publications/pguide/pguidee.htm

Kornblum, Janet (2006, Mar 8). How to monitor the kids from online social perils?. Retrieved Apr 24,2006, from USA Today–Tech Web site: http://www.usatoday.com/tech/news/internetprivacy/2006–03–08–generation–gap–x.htm

Reporting an incident. Retrieved Apr 24, 2006, from NetSafeKids Web site: http://www.nap.edu/netsafekids/pro_report.html

Safety tips–internet safety. Retrieved Apr 24, 2006, from Federal Bureau of Investigation Web site: http://www.fbi.gov/kids/k5th/safety2.htm

Setting rules for internet use–guidelines for parents. Retrieved Apr 24, 2006, from NetSafeKids Web site: http://www.nap.edu/netsafekids/pro_set_guidelines.html

Pamela Stevens

Pamela Stevens writes for TopTenREVIEWS.com, an online review service that publishes unbasied software, online service and hardware reviews. TopTenReviews also publishes movie reviews and entertainment pages. Please see http://www.toptenreviews.com for reviews and articles on a wide variety of topics.

MySpace, Facebook, Weblogs for Teenagers; What do Parents Need to Know?

By Sue Blaney

MySpace, Facebook, Xanga, LiveJournal…blogs, social networking… "What does this all mean?" parents wonder. "And do I really need to learn about this?"

The answer to the second question above is YES! Blogging sites are becoming increasingly popular with teenagers, and there are risks parents need to be aware of. Numerous school officials have had to take the lead in educating parents because online issues have spilled over into problems at school. Parents cannot sit in the dark any longer; we'll help you gain a better understanding of the issues starting here and now.

What it's about: The majority of your kids use the internet regularly; they socialize and communicate via Instant Messenger (IM), use the internet for research and homework, and almost half of them are at least looking at the popular "social networking" sites. MySpace, Facebook, LiveJournal and Xanga are the sites most often named, and while only 20% of kids 12 – 17* keep a blog there, over 40% of teens visit them regularly. MySpace is the largest of these sites, with around 42 million users. Users – often teens - post their profile which they customize with photos and descriptions of their interests, friends, favorite music, etc. Viewers can post messages to the user via the built-in messaging component, and the messages are visible for all to read. These sites usually require users to be of a certain [unenforceable] age, and to use the site according to their stated requirements.

When the user sets up his account he has several options to consider. One option is to set it up so that only invited visitors can leave messages. This means everyone who is not designated as a "friend" is only able to view this person's area, not interact with him. If this option is not selected, anyone can post messages to this user.

Take a look: Go to www.MySpace.com and browse around; it's not hard. You'll find some kids' pages are very sweet, indeed. This is a medium they understand; if you've never created a webpage you may find yourself in a new world, a world that our teenagers relate to. They choose the image they want to communicate by their choice of colors, layout, words and music. It can be rather charming, and many kids come across as sweet and honest. But nestled right next to the sweet naiveté you'll find some suggestive or raunchy pictures, profanity, and references that may upset you. Some kids – perhaps many kids - are misrepresenting their age, and promoting an image that might not be doing them any favors.

Teens' point of view: The odd issue here, is that many teenagers consider these areas to be private, and that parents and adults who visit these areas are invading their privacy. I've been told that I should "ask permission" to view a teenager's site. That anyone in the world can view their site seems to escape them completely. If and when you browse through these sites, be prepared for some resistance, particularly from older teens.

The issues for parents: What, exactly, do parents need to consider in this area that is generating so much discussion? The main issues are, as always, around safety. But as internet use also involves communication, appropriate social behavior, presenting one's image, and issues around freedom of expression, parents need to take a closer look. Exactly how you do that will be determined by your beliefs, communication style, your teenager's behavior, and the age of your teen.

Snooping vs Safety: If your child was in trouble would you go through his drawers to keep him safe? There comes a time where parental responsibility exceeds a child's right to privacy. Parents will need to use your best judgment in where that line lies and exactly how you address this issue.

Parents who established rules from the beginning about internet use and communication will have it easier as their kids have been taught that the computer is not a place free from supervision. Parents who made rules but didn't look over their kids' shoulders may run into this "privacy" cry head on. Don't be deterred because a lot is at stake today. Kids who post information they wouldn't want college recruiters, coaches, or potential employers to see can benefit from advice from knowledgeable adults.

If you've been telling your teenager that s/he cannot talk to strangers in chat rooms, you need to know that strangers may enter their space and initiate conversation in other ways unless they are blocked. Kids often misrepresent their age, but identify the school they attend. What they think is an untraceable posting is often anything but that. So parents have a responsibility to gain knowledge now and to act on that knowledge; being naïve can hurt your teen.

Posing, Posturing and Peer image: Adolescence is a time

when kids are formulating their self-image, a process which often includes some experimentation, trial and error. Much of this process is done in view of their peers, as teens try on different roles and personas. Although this developmental process can be confusing for parents, often this experimentation falls into "normal" bounds. Think of the current college scholar you know who dressed in all black as a high school freshman. Or the former preppy cheerleader who has relaxed her image as she dons her "Birks." Put into this context, posing as something they are not, may not be harmful or inherently bad. In fact, experimenting in cyberspace with an imaginary persona may feel more comfortable than experimenting in real life.

Take the boy who, on his weblog answered "Yes" to the question: "Did you get drunk last weekend?" When confronted, this 15 year old replied to his Mom that he "doesn't really drink," he just said that to be "cool." An 18 year old girl whom I know presents herself with a provocative pose on her MySpace page – definitely not projecting the shy girl I'm familiar with. She is fully clothed, and while nothing is inherently wrong in her photo, she projects an image quite different than the quiet persona she projects in person. Kids who experiment in this way may not be crossing the lines of acceptable behavior, although a parent may find it disturbing... and an opportunity for important discussion, at least.

Crossing the line: Posing as another person is all too common on the internet, and is often the cause of hurtful behavior. Kids have been known to send messages pretending they are somebody else, messages that cause unnecessary pain and misunderstanding. This is miscommunication at its worst, and it exemplifies some of the primary dangers of web communication. Maybe you've heard the term "Cyberbullying." This is worth learning about because it's happening in middle and high schools every day. Again, there's a role for parental intervention here if your teen has posed as someone else in their internet communication.

(For an excellent 2 minute video about these dangers go to NetSmartz.com and view the video "Cyberbullying and Broken Friendship.")

Real Dangers: Don't kid yourself that the dangers aren't real. Recent (February 2006) incidents with seven Connecticut teenagers has police investigating if the sexual assaults were the result of meetings initiated through MySpace.com. Predators can find it easy to obtain personal information – including telephone numbers and addresses – of kids who are listed on internet sites or participating anonymously in internet chat rooms.

(For an excellent short video demonstrating just how easy this is, go to NetSmartz.com and view "Tracking Teresa.")

The bottom line: Don't panic, but become informed. Parents should know about kids' actual activities in cyberspace. Ignorance is not an acceptable excuse. If your child has a posting on one of the weblogs she can probably use some guidance about appropriate ways to present herself to the world. It makes sense to discuss online communication and its consequences. Even older teens need to know that adults will be aware of what they present online, and the potential impact of this. These are not private areas.

Rules of your Home – Begin with Family Culture: What do you teach your kids about communicating with strangers? What do you teach them about appropriate language? Beth Fredericks, a parenting educator who has run internet safety classes says "Begin with your family culture. Keep rules of internet use consistent with all the other rules you've made for your family as they grow." Don't be intimidated by kids who claim this is their private area...there is nothing private about it.

Recommendations:

Keep the computer in an open family space, NOT in a child's bedroom.

Limit online time.

Be aware of how your child is spending her online time.

Educate your teens about internet realities – these areas are not private, and it is possible to trace users if they reveal even limited personal information.

Never talk in open chatrooms.

Never share your password or ask for the password from a friend.

Never pose as someone you are not.

When talking online, only say things that you would say if you were face-to face.

Resources:

isafe.org is an organization that provides information and training for parents and educators around internet safety. (Visit www.isafe.org to learn more about this free program.)

NetSmartz.org (www.NetSmartz.org) is another informational resource for parents and they offer worthwhile informational videos you can view online as well as other resources.

*from a study by the Pew Internet & American Life Project

Sue Blaney is the author of Please Stop the Rollercoaster! How Parents of Teenagers Can Smooth Out the Ride, and Practical Tips for Parents of Young Teens; What You Can Do to Enhance Your Child's Middle School Years. As a communications expert and the parent of two teenagers, she speaks frequently to parents, educators, and other professionals about parenting issues, improving communication, increasing parent involvement, and creating parent discussion groups. Visit her website at Please Stop the Rollercoaster and her blog at Parenting Teenagers.net

Online Safety Of Your Children Starts With You As A Parent

By Coenraad De Beer

Parental control software is far from perfect and your kids are smarter than you may think, they will always find a way around them. Companies developing this software make millions out of parents neglecting their responsibility as a parent. What is the use of restricting the access on their computer, if they can find other ways of accessing the sites they want? You cannot use a computer program to prevent them from watching indecent TV shows and movies, you cannot use a computer program to prevent them from reading indecent magazines and books, you cannot use a computer program to help them choose their friends or prevent them from using drugs, you cannot use a computer program to protect them from predators.

You, as a parent have the responsibility to educate your children, when they are old enough to understand, about what is right and what is wrong in life. Many kids buy their own books, computer games, they rent their own DVD's, some even have their own TV set, so it is useless, in fact foolish, to control only one source of bad influence on your children? You are only treating the symptoms and not the root of the problem and the root is lack of proper education and raising your children without good moral values. People do not take it serious when they are warned against the damaging effects of exposing children to all the explicit sex, nudity, violence and bad language through all the different mediums available to us today. When these immoral acts negatively affect adults and offend them, what effect do you think does it have on young children? I know that immoral material on the Internet sometimes make an appearance through unsuspected pop up windows, but these pop ups normally appear on sites where children should not have been in the first place. Our moral values have degraded so much that indecent web sites are not seen as "bad" anymore. The adults consuming this content today are the product of a previous generation of people who threw all moral values overboard.

The online safety of your children is not only about maintaining high moral values, it is also about keeping them away from online predators. These people are active on IRC channels (chat rooms), forums and may even contact your child via e-mail. So many teenagers have walked into the trap of deception. There is no way of verifying the identity of the person on the other side of your computer screen. An adult online predator, pretending to be a teenager, can easily mislead your teenager into believing that he/she has found a good online friend. This is why online dating is so dangerous, not only for children but adults as well. Online predators can behave well, they can be friendly and kind, they can be sympathetic to the problems of your child and you child can easily find comfort in that. Never let your child meet an online friend without your presence and tell them how dangerous it is meeting or talking to total strangers without parental guidance.

Educate your children not to give personal details, addresses and telephone numbers to anyone online, you should determine whether it is safe to provide these details by assessing the situation. There may be circumstances where these details are required for subscriptions to safe online services your child might want to use. You should be the judge of which services are suitable for your children and which ones are not. If you are unsure of the safety of a certain service, ask for the opinion of an expert or someone else already using it. Do not give your children too much power if they cannot use it responsible, too much control is not good either and you should find a balance between the two. If you fail to find a balance, you will end up compromising the safety of your child in the online and as well as the offline world.

Trust goes both ways and the trust showed by the one party will help win the trust of the other party. You need to be able to trust your children, trusting that they will stick to the rules you make. You should make it clear what the consequences will be if they disobey and misbehave, be consequent with your actions and make no exceptions to your own rules. They should also be able to trust you, knowing that you will not invade their privacy. Breaking into their e-mail accounts and reading their e-mails, or installing spyware to spy on their online activities is not the right way of protecting your children. Both parties should be open and honest towards each other with everything they do. Your child should have enough confidence in you, to turn to you when he or she is unsure of something or did something wrong. Not taking your child serious in such a case will break down the trust built up between the two of you and you will end up being the direct cause of his or her mistakes. Children are a gift from God, never neglect your responsibility as a parent.

ABOUT THE AUTHOR

Coenraad is webmaster and founder of Cyber Top Cops,

leaders in Internet security, prevention of online fraud
and educating users against online scams and malicious
software.

Keeping Children Safe On The Internet

By Anne Clarke

You hear about it on the news, in the papers and in magazines. There are hundreds of crimes that happen every day because of children using the Internet. Predators take advantage of children because they are often trusting and easy to fool. Therefore they become vulnerable and are easy victims for criminals, kidnappers, child molesters and even killers.

The following are some basic rules for your child to follow in order to promote safety on the Internet:

These rules are very important for children not just to know of, but also to memorize. And keep in mind that it is not just the kids. We could all become victims of violent crimes that begin online.

a) Let children know to always tell a grown-up when they get an uncomfortable feeling while online:

To promote child safety on the Internet, a child should know to be extremely cautious and always tell his or her parent(s) or guardian(s) what makes them uneasy. And at school, of course, children should inform their teachers too.

b) Teach your children that it is extremely dangerous to

give personal information to anyone online—absolutely never. Please stress this rule most of all:

Children should not give information such as his or her address, phone number, name, school, photo of him or herself, or his or her favorite hangouts. Even if the person seems nice and will provide all of the same information about him or herself. Your child must know that there will be no "switching of information" between online "friends"

Explain to the child or children that although it may really seem unfair, this is a very important rule. Unfortunately, this rule does take away from children making real connections with honest and trustworthy friends. It is sad but true, what's more—is it is scary.

It could become dangerous for you child to simply even go to the mall if a predator knows that he or she likes to frequent "The Gap" or knows someone who works at the jewelry and accessories boutique, etc.

c) No contact:

Children must know to prevent any harm against them by NEVER, EVER meeting with someone they met first online. Even if the place he or she chooses to meet with this mysterious person is in out in the open—it can still be a very dangerous move.

I have read about many cases where an adult removes (or in more accurate terms—kidnaps) a screaming child from a store, park, shopping mall etc. One rule I have learned regarding such a case is to tell the children to scream out: "you are not my mommy!" or something similar. This will actually have more of an impact on other people and perhaps even catch their attention in enough time to stop the criminal.

If there is a rare case—after carefully monitoring the communications between them, perhaps a meeting could be possible. However, an adult should accompany the child. And perhaps speak with the stranger's parents on the phone before hand—BUT STILL BE THERE! Pessimistic as it may be, bring a cell phone along and be ready to call 911.

d) Ask an adult:

A child should always ask before doing anything especially significant. Downloading, installing software, opening odd emails etc. is dangerous because these things may compromise the privacy of personal information.

Children need to know to always, always, always ask an adult before going online. Even if this means that parents have to restrict or block Internet access while they are not at home.

The same thing should be done in school. For example: the computers may not be accessible when the children want to use them without adult supervision. Thank goodness most schools have someone to observe computer labs shared by many different students for both schoolwork and homework.

e) Most importantly, the child should be aware of the seriousness of these restrictions:

If a child does not take these rules seriously he or she may already be in danger. No matter what other rules your students or children ignore—these rules cannot be among them. Breaking these rules could be fatal!

For child safety on the Internet we must teach and reinforce all of these rules, repetition never hurts. Teachers, do not assume they will learn these lessons at home; parent(s) or guardian(s): never assume these rules will be taught in school (although they should be without question). The basic guidelines for child safety on the Internet that I have just laid out are literally tools for preventing heinous crimes. Recognize that these potential dangers are everywhere on the web.

As technology advances more and more, the rules laid out above become even more important.

Anne Clarke writes numerous articles for websites on gardening, parenting, fashion, and home decor. Her background includes teaching and gardening. For more of her articles about online safety please visit Internet Safety.

Chat Rooms and Internet Safety for Your Kids and Teens

By Eriani Doyel

Chat rooms are very popular with kids and teens right now. Sites like myspace.com and others can be a great way for kids to get to know other kids and teens who share the same interests as them. But, just as with nearly every other good thing, chat rooms have a dangerous side as well. Online predators, harassment, inappropriate language and other concerns can all be found in chat rooms that cater to kids and teens. So, before your children get online, you need to make sure that they understand all of the rules on the information highway.

Suggestions for Parents:

1. One of the best things that you can do to monitor your child's use of chat rooms is to have your computer in a public place. This will not only give you an easy way to check what they are doing, but you can limit their time online as well.

2. Since you cannot be watching your children constantly while they are online using chat rooms, you can purchase a software program that will monitor their use. Some programs can record "conversa-

tions," limit your child's time online, and even prevent your child from sharing personal information.

3. Have a discussion with your child to let them know the rules and then post the rules for using chat rooms and the internet. Make sure they understand and agree to all of the rules.

4. Get your child's login name and password for any chat rooms that they visit.

Rules for kids:

1. Never tell anyone what you look like, where you live, what your phone number is, or give out your full name.

2. Only use rooms that have a moderator.

3. If you see any language, pictures, etc. that are inappropriate or mean, talk to your parents or contact the moderator immediately.

4. Don't agree to meet anyone you meet online without permission from your parents.

5. Don't send your picture or anything else to anyone you meet online unless your parents agree.

6. Never give out your password or login information to anyone except your parents.

7. Ask permission before you have a "private chat" or IM.

Eriani Doyel writes articles about Chat Rooms. For more information about chat rooms visit www.figarden.com

Online Resources for Internet Safety

Safekids.com

NetSmartz.org

TodaysParent.com

KidsBeSafeOnline.com

SafeCanada.ca

WiredKids.org

NetSmartzKids.org

KidsHealth.org

ProtectKids.org

CyberAngels.org

KidSmart.org.uk

iSafe.org

FamilyInternet.About.com

Kids.gov

NetSafe.org

WiredSafety.org

ProtectKids.com

Safe2Read.com

WiredWithWisdom.org

iKeepSafe.com

ResponsibleKids.net

The Internet Glossary

A definition of common internet terms

Adware: Software on your computer that displays advertisements that you cannot control.

ASAP: As soon as possible

A/S/L?: Age/sex/location?

BF: Boyfriend

Blog: Web log, an online journal.

Bookmarks: Pages saved in your browser for later reference.

BRB: Be right back.

Browser: The program you use to view websites on the internet.

BTW: By the way

Chat: Instant conversation over the internet, usually in a large group.

Cookies: Bits of information that the websites you visit store on your computer for later use.

CU: See you.

Directory: A list of websites categorized in an easy to navigate manner.

Domain: How a website is located. Examples include Google.com or MSN.com

Download: Bringing a file from the internet and saving it on your computer for later use.

Email: Electronic mail, sent over the internet from one user to another.

Encryption: Protection of your data during transmission over the internet etc. Often used when logging into websites.

F2F: Face to face

FAQ: Frequently asked questions

File-Sharing: The use of software that allows other users to download files from your computer, while allowing you to download files from theirs. Often used to illegally download music.

Filtering Tools: Software on your computer that "filters out" content or files that may not be suitable for your viewing.

Firewall: Software that protects your computer by limiting who can "come in and go out" through your internet access.

Flame: Insult or negative comment about someone in a chat room or forum.

Flame War: Series of flames in which there is no longer a real discussion, just an exchange of random insults.

FYI: For your information.

GF: Girlfriend

History: Files automatically stored by your browser so that you can go back to pages you have previously visited.

HTML: HyperText Markup Language, the language that web pages and websites are coded in.

IC: I see.

IM: Instant message.

IMHO: In my humble opinion.

Instant Messaging (IM): Chatting one-on-one through an instant message program such as IRC or MSN.

Internet: A network consisting of hundreds of smaller networks that allow you to access any information on the World Wide Web.

Internet Service Provider (ISP): The company that provides the service that connects you to the internet, such as AOL.

IP Address: This is the "address" of your computer, much like "123 Any St." would be the address of your house.

IRL: In real life.

JK: Joking / Just Kidding

K: Okay

L8R: Later

LOL: Laughing out loud

Mirror: Often a term used when downloading, it is another location on the internet for the exact same content or file.

Netiquette: Etiquette on the internet.

Netizen: A citizen or user on the internet.

NP or N/P: No problem.

OIC: Oh, I see.

OMG: Oh my goodness.

PDA: Public display of affection.

PM: Private Message

Pod-Casting: The broadcasting of downloadable audio files on the internet, often for use on an MP3 player.

QT: Cutie.

ROTFL: Rolling on the floor laughing.

RSS: Really Simple Syndication. A way of reading updated news from websites or blogs without having to visit them.

Search Engine: Allows you to search the internet for information you are looking for. Examples include Google and Ask Jeeves

Spam: Unsolicited email, usually involving the sale or promotion of a product.

Spyware: Software on your computer that tracks your activities and sends the information back to the program designer.

THX: Thanks.

TMI: Too much information.

Trojan: A type of virus that creates a virtual "back door" into your computer, letting hackers access it any time they like.

TTFN: Ta-ta for now.

TTYL: Talk to you later.

URL: Uniform Resource Locater. This is what you type into your browser to reach a specific website. Examples include www.Google.com and www.MSN.com, but can also include links like http://www.google.com/search?hl=en&q=search – This is also a URL.

WB: Welcome back. Often used in chat rooms when someone leaves and then re-enters the room during conversation.

Virus: A piece of software installed on your computer that compromises security and causes your computer to act in a way you did not intent.

VOIP: Voice Over Internet Protocol. Technology now being used to make phone calls over the internet.

Popular Scam Emails

This is a list of commonly circulated emails involving scams or false warnings/alerts. Source: Snopes.com

Here is one commonly circulated email about Glade brand Plug-Ins.

"Subject : Electrical Hazard

My brother and his wife learned a hard lesson this last week. Their house burned down... nothing left but ashes. They have good insurance, so the home will be replaced and most of the contents. That is the good news. However, they were sick when they found out the cause of the fire.

The insurance investigator sifted through the ashes for several hours. He had the cause of the fire traced to the master bathroom. He asked my sister-in-law what she had plugged in the bathroom. She listed the normal things... curling iron, blow dryer. He kept saying to her, "No, this would be something that would disintegrate at high temperatures." Then, my sister-in-law remembered she had a Glade Plug-in in the bathroom. The investigator had one of those "Aha" moments. He said that was the cause of the fire. He has seen more home fires started with the plug in type room fresheners than anything else. He said the plastic they are made from is a THIN plastic. He said in every case there was nothing left to prove that it even existed. When the investigator looked in the wall plug, the two prongs left from the plug-in were still in there.

My sister-in-law had one of the plug-ins that had a small night light built in it. She said she had noticed that the light would dim... and then finally go out. She would walk in a few hours later, and the light would be back on again. The investigator said that the unit was getting too hot, and would dim and go out rather than just blow the light bulb. Once it cooled down, it would come back on. That is a warning sign. The investigator said he personally wouldn't have any type of plug in fragrance device anywhere in his house. He has seen too many burned down homes.

Thought I would warn you all. I had several of them plugged in my house. I immediately took them all down."

Of course, this email warning is false. Glade Plug-ins will not make your house burn down.

Here is another email that is circulated widely, telling all cell phone users to register their phone number with the national "Do Not Call" registry to avoid having telemarketers call their cell phones.

"Subject : Warning! Pass this on...

Greetings To All of My Friends and Family

In just 4 days from today all U.S. cell phone numbers will be released to telemarketing companies and you will begin to receive sales calls. You will be charged for these calls! Even if you do not answer, the telemarketer will end up in your voice mail and you will be charged for all of the minutes the incoming (usually recorded) message takes to complete. You will then also be charged when you call your voice mail to retrieve your messages.

To prevent this, call 888-382-1222 from your cell phone. This is the national DO NOT CALL list; it takes only a minute to register your cell phone number and it blocks most telemarketers calls for five years.

In case you have friends other than me, pass this on to them."

Of course this is entirely false. First, the national cellular phone 411 registry, while it does exist, is something you have to ASK to be included in. Second, the only people that have access to this list are 411 operators. Third, it is illegal for telemarketers to use auto-dialers to dial cell phone numbers. Fourth, you are never charged for an incoming voice mail message. You are only ever charged for incoming voicemail IF you dial your voicemail from your cellular phone.

Here is an email that claims certain brands of lipstick contain cancer-causing lead.

"Subject : Beware! Lipstick contains LEAD!!

This is how to test lipstick for "lead", lead is a chemical which causes cancer. Recently a brand called "Red Earth" decreased their prices from HK$67 to HK$9.9. It contains lead.

Brands which contain Lead

1.   Christian Dior 4

2.   LANCOME 2

3.   CLINIQUE 2

4. Y.S.L. 5

5. ESTEE LAUDER 3

6. SHISEIDO 2

7. RED EARTH (Lip Gloss) 2

8. CHANEL (Lip Conditioner) 2

9. Market America-Motives lipstick 0

The higher the number of lead the higher the content which means a greater chance of causing Cancer. After doing this test, we found Y.S.L. lipstick to contain the most lead. It is not easy to "REMOVE" because of the lead. Watch out for those lipsticks which are supposed to stay longer

Here is the test you can do yourself:

1. Put some lipstick on your hand,

2. Use a 24k-14k Gold ring to scratch on the lipstick.

3. If the lipstick color changes to black then you know the lipstick contains lead.

Please send this information to all your girl friends."

Of course, while there are tiny grains of truth throughout the email, they are all modified in such a way as to create panic and fear. First, it would be illegal for lipstick in the U.S. to contain lead, the FDA makes sure of that. Second, lead exposure doesn't cause cancer even in the highest dosages. Third, scratching many kinds of metal on any surface (not just one coated in lipstick) will often cause a gray or brown streak to appear.

Here is one email that will reportedly make you thousands of dollars just by forwarding it around, all on Bill Gates' tab.

"Subject : Sounds Pretty Simple... Need Money?

Sent: February 11, 2002 10:24 AM

Subject: Fw: THIS IS NOT JUNK LETTER. BILL GATES IS SHARING HIS FORTUNE.

Dear Friends,

Please do not take this for a junk letter. Bill Gates is sharing his fortune. If you ignore this you will repent later. Microsoft and AOL are now the largest Internet companies and in an effort to make sure that Internet Explorer remains the most widely used program, Microsoft and AOL are running an e-mail beta test.

When you forward this e-mail to friends, Microsoft can and will track it (if you are a Microsoft Windows user) for a two week time period. For every person that you forward this e-mail to, Microsoft will pay you $245.00, for every person that you sent it to that forwards it on, Microsoft will pay you $243.00 and for every third person that receives it, you will be paid $241.00. Within two weeks, Microsoft will contact you for your address and then send you a check.

Regards. Chinu! I thought this was a scam myself, but two weeks after receiving this e-mail and forwarding it on, Microsoft contacted me for my address and within days, I received a check for US$24,800.00. You need to respond before the beta testing is over. If anyone can afford this Bill Gates is the man. It's all marketing expense to him. Please forward this to as many people as possible. You are bound to get at least US$10,000.00."

Of course, Bill Gates would do no such thing. Here is an excerpt from "On Spam: Wasting Time on the Internet."

Even more annoying than spam, in some respects, are hoaxes. I'm acutely aware of this because my name was recently attached to a hoax email message that was widely distributed.

People embellished the fraudulent email over time, as it was forwarded from electronic mailbox to electronic mailbox, but an early version read this way:

"My name is Bill Gates. I have just written up an e-mail tracing program that traces everyone to whom this message is forwarded to. I am experimenting with this and I need your help. Forward this to everyone you know and if it reaches 1000 people everyone on the list will receive $1000 at my expense. Enjoy. Your friend, Bill Gates."

The bogus message was widely forwarded, which surely led to some disappointment from people who hoped to receive $1,000 for passing along what was essentially a chain letter.

Who do you think wrote that? Yep, none other than Bill Gates himself. Use your common sense with things like this. If you were Bill Gates, would you give a couple thousand dollars to everyone who forwarded an email? No, you would rather rent a yacht and go sailing around Aruba or Mexico.

For your reading pleasure, here is one final email hoax. It claims that using plastic wrap to microwave your food will cause "Dioxin" to be released into the food and give you cancer. Yeah, right.

"Subject: Dioxins

From a Concerned Friend

Passing on healthy info.

I just wanted to pass some information on to you. I was watching Channel 2 this morning. They had a Dr. Edward Fujimoto from Castle Hospital on the program. He is the manager of the Wellness Program at the hospital. He was talking about dioxins and how bad they are for us. He said that we should not be heating our food in the microwave using plastic containers. This applies to foods that contain fat. He said that the combination of fat, high heat and plastics releases dioxins into the food and ultimately into the cells of the body. Dioxins are carcinogens and highly toxic to the cells of our bodies.

Instead, he recommends using glass, Corning Ware, or ceramic containers for heating food. You get the same results without the dioxins. So such things as TV dinners, instant saimin and soups, etc. should be removed from the container and heated in something else.

Paper isn't bad but you don't know what is in the paper. Just safer to use tempered glass, Corning Ware, etc. He said we might remember when some of the fast food restaurants moved away from the foam containers to paper. The dioxin problem is one of the reasons.

Past this on to your friends."

Now obviously this isn't true. Dioxins CAN be produced if large quantities of PVC are incinerated at extremely high temperatures. How this translates into plastic wrap in the microwave, no one will ever know.

Popular Social Networking Sites

A list of popular social networking sites is included below. They are sorted by the most popular (meaning the most estimated users), from highest to lowest. Source : Wikipedia. org

MySpace

Hi5

orkut

Classmates.com

Xanga

Windows Live Spaces

Friendster

Reunion.com

Bebo

BlackPlanet.com

Facebook

Cyworld

Friends Reunite

Facebox

LiveJournal

Piczo
LinkedIn
Mixi
WAYN (Where are you now?)
Care2
Faceparty
Gaia Online
Yahoo! 360*
Passado
Bolt
Flickr
eCRUSH
MiGente.com
Multiply
Hyves
TagWorld
CarDomain
GreatestJournal
iWiW
Rediff Connexions
myGamma
LunarStorm
Stumbleupon
Stuivz
IMVU
XING
Xuqa
Fotki

myYearbook

Blurty

Nexopia

Grono.net

The Student Center

Vampire Freaks

Neurona

Draugiem.lv

Graduates.com

43 Things

Tribe

Playahead

Sconex

DeadJournal

GoPets

Threadless

IRC-Galleria

Ruckus

Ryze

DontStayIn

asmallWorld

TakingITGlobal

ProfileHeaven

Ecademy

Phrasebase

Travellerspoint

Blue Dot

MEETin

Doostang
Zaadz
Studybreakers
Babbello
Consumating
VietSpace
Advogato
Fruhstuckstreff
youBlab.com
Dandelife
Gazzag
MOG
Vox
Mugshot
Yelp
Last.fm
LDS Singles Hearts
WebBiographics
Joga Bonito
imeem
Dodgeball.com

Conclusion

A final word on internet safety

DON'T BELIEVE EVERYTHING YOU READ

If nothing else, that is most important. You are an intelligent young adult, on the verge of a new kind of society. Everything is becoming more and more digitized and less and less information is available "offline". Your most important tool of defense on the internet is common sense. If it sounds too good to be true, or feels wrong, it probably is. You are smart enough to know the difference.

WHAT TO DO IF THIS HAPPENS TO YOU

You may be wondering at this point what to do if any of this happens to you. It is fairly simple, really. Your first line of defense lies right on your computer. The delete key, or the close button, is your "front-lines" in the fight for internet safety. Use these tools wisely, and you will rarely need to go farther. However, if someone or something begins to bother you, never hesitate to tell a responsible adult that you trust. This can be a parent, a teacher, a counselor, or even an older sibling. Remember that everyone will be much happier to know if something is happening now, than potentially learning too late.

Your parents have been well educated by the media on how to best protect you, and one of the core lessons taught to your parents is to be reasonable and understanding when you need their help. They know that "freaking out" isn't going to resolve the situation, and understand that you are coming to them looking for help. They are prepared, whether you would like to think that or not.

There is a resource that can help you if you do not feel comfortable talking to an adult you know about your situation. They are known as the CyberAngels, and have been helping victims of internet crimes confidentially for over 10 years. Established in 1995, the CyberAngels make it their mission to educate the public about internet crimes and to help protect and counsel those who are already victims. You can visit the CyberAngels at www.CyberAngels.org.